PATHOLOGICAL CHRISTIANITY

The Dangers and Cures of Extremist Fundamentalisms

PATHOLOGICAL CHRISTIANITY

The Dangers and Cures of
Extremist Fundamentalisms

Gregory Max Vogt, Ph.D.

Cross Cultural Publications, Inc.
CrossRoads Books

Published by **CROSS CULTURAL PUBLICATIONS, INC.**
CROSS ROADS BOOKS
Post Office Box 506
Notre Dame, Indiana, 46556, U.S.A.
Phone: (219) 272-0889
FAX: (219) 273-5973

©1995 CROSS CULTURAL PUBLICATIONS, INC.
All Rights Reserved
 ISBN: 0-940121-31-x
Library of Congress Catalog Card Number: 94-71587

Pathological Christianity:

The Dangers and Cures
Of Extremist Fundamentalisms

Gregory Max Vogt, Ph.D.

CONTENTS

Chapter 1. **Painful Changes**

TED AND MARJORIE SAT AT OPPOSITE ends of the couch in my office. They were both telling the same story, but his view of it was far different than hers. She was looking at me, smiling and sometimes crying as she told the story of "Ted and Marjorie, The Perfect Couple."

Ted had been scowling and looking at his shoes. Suddenly, he flashed at Marjorie, "We *were* the perfect couple. What's wrong with that? We still could be the perfect couple, if..."

Marjorie interrupted. "If only I would give up all my crazy notions, all this nonsense I have been spouting, and come back and make our life the way it used to be."

"Was it so horrible as all that?" asked Ted. "Haven't you always had everything you asked for?" He was trying hard to make a point, and it was clear that he honestly believed he had done what he was supposed to do and now he felt confused and betrayed by Marjorie.

Marjorie answered, "Ted, I really do appreciate what you have done to provide for us in your work, your careful attention to money. You are an excellent provider. You are not a bad guy. You are a good man, but you have to understand that what you call our life together feels to me now like being buried alive. I cannot simply lie down in that hole anymore and have the dirt shoveled on me. I cannot live what you call the Christian Life anymore, Ted. It is so utterly fake and sterile. I cannot go around being a dutiful Christian woman anymore, and I can't bear the thought of our daughter thinking the way I have acted is the only acceptable way for a woman to be in this world."

"You have been a great mother!" Ted was beginning to heat up. "Until now, that is. Now I don't know what you are."

"To tell you the truth, I don't know what I am either," grinned Marjorie. "And the thought of living without any particular role to play or ideal to fulfill or expectations of yours or the Church's to meet, that whole new approach to life excites me no end."

"Well, I guess that is all that matters, then," sputtered Ted. "Your excitement, your new life, your graduate degree, your psychotherapy." At this point he glared at me and then back at her. I was not her psychotherapist, but I guess I served as a stand-in for the moment. "Isn't that all terribly selfish and petty? Don't you remember the sacred vows and the promises you made to me and to the Church and to Jesus Christ? Are you prepared to take the consequences of being a liar and a traitor to the Lord?"

Marjorie was silent for a while and looked down into her lap. Then she looked at Ted and spoke softly. "Ted, I don't want to hurt you. I never wanted to leave you and even now I would far prefer not to. I still love you in some ways and even though you have accused me of being with another man, it is simply not true. All I wanted my whole adult life was to love you, to make a home with you, to grow in Christ with you all our lives, and go to Heaven and know you forever in God. You had lots of affairs, but I never minded so much. You never paid much attention to your daughter and are disappointed that I gave you no male heirs. Don't deny it here, please!"

"I kept myself busy all these years, thinking that once you made a success of yourself, you and I could become good friends. But you have never been interested in anything about me, other than how well I conform to your ideal of a Christian Woman."

Ted held up his hand, palm out, in front of Marjorie. "Please," he said. "Marjorie, you are the only woman I have ever loved. I have prayed using your name every day. Christ has blessed our life together in every conceivable way. You cannot break that up, you must not break that up."

"What you don't seem willing to see, Ted, and what you have once again proven to me in this moment by what you are doing right now, is that you will not be my friend. You only want to be my preacher, to tell me how I should act and why I should act that way. I don't want a friend, lover or husband who takes that attitude to me ever again. I no longer have a need to have a husband just to say I have one, so I can feel good and clean and righteous. I am done with that, Ted."

"I am friendly to you," Ted whined.

"You are not friendly," Marjorie spoke. "You do not listen to my ideas thoughtfully or respectfully. I am not crazy, I am not a sinner as you so often have said to me, and I am not about to feel guilty for thinking my own thoughts and feeling my own feelings. I know how you think and feel. You have made it exquisitely clear to me. I have never demanded that you feel and think otherwise, though I have in the last ten years tried to discuss your views with you, for which I get nothing but your scorn. I simply have wanted you to keep your mind open for change."

"But you know I can't do that," replied Ted. "Christ has called me, called me to live by his ways. I can love you as Christ loves the Church, and because of that love, I must insist that you live the Christian life."

"That is not a friendship or a marriage but an imprisonment. It is not an attitude of love at all, but one of political tyranny, Ted."

"MARJORIE!" suddenly Ted boomed out, waving his index finger in the air. "In GOD'S NAME, I COMMAND YOU TO COME BACK TO THE HOUSE, AND TO BRING MELISSA WITH YOU--NOW! TODAY!"

I was not expecting this abrupt outburst from Ted, and I am afraid my head snapped back a little in alarm. Marjorie saw my reaction and giggled a little, and then turned to Ted. "Ted, you don't scare me with that crap any more, although I am afraid you got a little rise from Dr. Vogt. That kind of intensity doesn't work with me now. I don't belong to you now or ever, though I am sorry I once did think so and must have led you on. The reason I asked you to meet with Dr. Vogt was because I hoped we would be able to begin saying good-bye to each other in a loving and respectful way."

"And the only reason I came," replied Ted, who was panting and wide-eyed from the energy of his pronouncement. "Was to try to talk you into coming back, into doing the right thing by staying in the marriage."

"It is all over," said Marjorie. "Done with. I don't know why I thought you might be more available to say good-bye to me in a meaningful way when you never expressed any emotional interest in me in the first place during all those years we were together. It is just difficult to give up the fantasy that things are going to turn out all right."

Both Ted and Marjorie have been and continue to be victims of a way of life and assumptions about life that harmed them and hampered their development into psychologically mature human beings. Marjorie seemed free, but was crying for all she had lost by living a false way of life. She still longed for a friendship and understanding with Ted, which she had to begin recognizing was not going to happen. Later in the session, she admitted that despite her bravado, she still felt guilty and ashamed for thinking for herself, and for wanting more depth in a relationship with a man than Ted would offer. She said that she still was anticipating somewhere deep inside some punishment from God for "rebelling" against Ted's expectations of her and for bucking her pastor in filing for divorce. She knew she was not crazy or weird or tempted by the devil. She had not, as Ted implied, "lost her faith," but felt strengthened in her spirituality. Ted scoffed at this notion, asking her if she had "joined a witch's coven yet." Marjorie told me that this comment arose from the fact that she had been studying the old goddess religions as part of her graduate studies and Ted thought because of her interest she was getting ready to become a witch. She said that Ted accused her and her professors of all sorts of heresies because they claimed that the beliefs and codes of conduct for parishioners in Ted's church were simply white, middle-class American social mores and bore no absolute claims to be founded in the Bible or any other Christian tradition at all.

Marjorie was just beginning to get free of the fetters Pathological Christianity, and to discover a responsible psychological maturity based on critical thinking and critical feeling rather than on fear and superstition. She still considered herself very much a Christian, and felt that some of the teachings ascribed to Jesus would always be important to her. More importantly, though, she felt that the whole question was becoming less vital to her as she found that life was about far more than the narrow teachings she had lived under all her life.

Ted was hurt but stoical and far from being able to recognize the harm Pathological Christianity had inflicted on him. He was very trapped by his beliefs. He refused to see that he had lost his wife and daughter, whom he really did cherish, because he refused to move from his rigid positions about life, "the family" and the roles of men and women. He felt bad, he admitted, and had felt bad all his life because he had not been able to live up to his own "Christian expectations." Yet when Marjorie asked him if he saw the paradox this put him in and whether there might not be something wrong in those expectations themselves, he flatly denied it, reiterating that it was only his sinful nature which caused him problems. Ted was not enjoying life and all he believed in was unraveling before him, but his reaction was only to tighten up more. By the end of the session, he was telling me that I was "abetting sin" by encouraging Marjorie to divorce him. The truth was that I had barely gotten a word in myself either of encouragement or any other attitude toward Ted or Marjorie. However, I guess he must have sensed that I felt some support for Marjorie in her struggle to think and feel for herself. But I also felt a profound compassion for him in his pain and confusion.

The subtitle of this book is *The Dangers and Cures of Extremist Fundamentalisms.* Ted was no raving extremist. He looked about as much like a terrorist as Mister Rogers in his cardigan sweater. Yet he was a tyrant and a kind of terrorist despite his benign demeanor, because of the approach to life he supported, and which is the topic of this book. A middle-aged man, Ted looked hearty and fit. He sat upright in the chair across from me in my therapy office, working hard to keep his composure and his strongly held position. Really, he was very likable and well-meaning. He had worked hard all his life and could not see any value in how things were turning out for him. His world was falling apart and he was feeling deeply hurt.

Ted was on a mission. His life was not turning out the way he had planned it or in his words, according to God's plan, and he already knew why. He knew who was to blame and what needed to be done. His certainty about this other person's complete guilt in ruining his life was only matched by his indignation over her refusal to agree with him or with "God's will." This other person, his wife Marjorie, had left him and taken their daughter with her. She was being rebellious, sinful and turning her back on God, he claimed. Ted felt betrayed, confused, angry, and was looking for some way to make everything change back to the way it was before Marjorie left.

It is not unusual for men or women in divorce to blame one another out of their deep disappointment, anger or feeling of failure. Actually all biological organisms from single-cell protozoa to humans try to avoid discomfort by the maneuver of shifting what makes them uncomfortable to others and by gathering around them what makes them comfortable including others of like kind. But organisms also tend to explore the unknown and push into new territory often with negative consequences from the environment or from others of like kind. Whenever humans go through rapid and sweeping social changes as we are in the latter half of our century, there are bound to be forces that try to push us back to the way things once were. Fundamentalism as an attitude toward life in general is this kind of force, the attempt to push things back into the familiar and to resist changes.

The vast challenges to American life that are taking place are very threatening to many people. They see the "American way of life" shattered and broken. Among those most threatened are the groups who identify themselves as Evangelical Christians or Fundamentalist Christians. They go by many names, but their principal point of agreement is that God has specific requirements of people on earth and that they are stated in the Bible if one reads it as God demands it be read. There are some slight differences in vehemence or insistence on particular behaviors, but essentially all American Evangelical Christians agree that the white American middle-class model of the family practiced in the years immediately following World War II is the only way of life sanctioned by God.

And here sat Ted in front of me carrying the weight of all those expectations. He believed he had done right and now should receive his well-deserved reward from God and from his wife Marjorie and the kids.

She had decided to divorce him, and he just could not understand why; certainly he had no blame for this sinful decision. He had always been a good Christian man, he said. They had the life Ted's parents had only dreamed of, a lovely house and yard, not far from being paid off. Their daughter Melissa attended a good private Christian high school, to which he contributed a substantial amount of his large income. He was an accomplished engineer who also had some inventions and patents. Marjorie had been active at the church and in Bible study, in the parents groups in school, in several community organizations and had finished a Master's Degree in Religious Studies from a Christian university where she commuted.

When I first spoke to him on the phone about coming in, Ted was scouting me out to see if I "used Biblical Principles" in my practice. I knew what he was fishing for. These are code words in evangelical-style Christian Counseling for the acceptance and insistence on certain universal rules for thought, feeling and behavior. They are rules based on post-World War

II White American middle class values about family, home and the roles of men, women and children. He wanted to know if I would join up with him to blackmail his wife into giving up her request for divorce. He wanted to know if I would team up with him and use my leverage and credentials to convince her that she was committing sin by asking for divorce, and that she must give up her decisions and actions and come back to him and conform to what his preacher had commanded her to do. The pastor of their church believed in and practiced a severe form of ostracism from the church for parishioners who did not conform to "Biblical Principles." I told him I was brought up Christian, but I didn't know if his interpretation of the Bible would match mine, though I thought perhaps it would not. I reminded him of his right to choose whatever counselor he wanted to go to, or not to go at all, but said that Marjorie had invited him to meet with me and I needed to know whether to put him on the schedule or not. He reluctantly agreed to come in.

It is very understandable why people join fundamentalist causes, whether religious, social or political. Change is difficult and frightening, and freedom combined with change can wreak havoc for a while.

The source of problems in the contemporary world is not that people have freedom but that we have no idea what to do with all this freedom we have in the light of all the guilt and blame we are trained to feel about our very being. The problem is not freedom but millennia of enslavement. It will take us time, much more time than we've been working on the problem of freedom, to know how to handle our capacity to think and feel on our own in such a way that is effective. But first we must recognize that the fears we feel when we discover that we are really free are superstitions. Then we will find ways of managing and understanding our freedoms responsibly and without the need for the threats of divine punishment as the yokes for keeping us in control.

When I was a kid, there was a mean old guy who lived down the road a way. He had a lot of dogs on his farm. Most of them he kept in cages and he treated all of them badly. One dog in particular, a female Brittany spaniel, he held in some kind of peculiar hatred. He whipped and kicked and tortured that dog and almost never fed her, and she used to howl and moan day and night. Then suddenly one night an ambulance came for the old man, and he died. When my friends and I heard the old man died, the first thing we did was to go over to his place and try to let those dogs go, especially the beautiful Brittany spaniel. But she wouldn't leave her cage; she was too afraid. She just stood in the cage and shook in terror.

We worked with that dog for several weeks, trying to coax her out of her cage.. When she did finally leave her cage and play for a while, if any of us made any sudden move or raised our voice, she would rip a trail to her cage. For a long time she was gun-shy, suspicious, fearful; she wouldn't romp. We tried to hunt with her, but she would freeze up.

Then she got a little bolder and would go in the fields with us. During this time, she wouldn't mind at all and wouldn't come when we called her, but just took off through the fields and the barn and the house whenever and wherever she could, tearing up everything in sight.

She wouldn't sleep inside a dog house even on the coldest of nights, but out under the stars, shaking with the cold of winter, but free. I had the fantasy she loved the cold stars because they stood for freedom. Then the next year, suddenly she was a good hunting dog. She had decided to work with us. She came when we called, and worked the fields the best of any dog we'd ever seen. She was a fine hunter, a lively, skilled "craftsman." But one thing stuck from the old days. If we even raised our voice to her or lifted a hand suddenly over her head (meaning only to pet her), she ran and hid and we couldn't find her.

Only by a loving relationship could we deal with this dog who had once been so abused and humiliated; only by giving and taking and by showing our good will did she come around. But she was eventually the best hunter and the greatest spirit we ever saw because we took the patience and time that it took to come to her as a friend in respect for her being and her skill; nevermore would just raw discipline work with this dog.

This is the same situation we are in with our society, and particularly with parents and kids. We have come too far as a culture and as a world civilization to return to primitive and small-minded discipline as a way of guiding and forming excellence in our young people. Kids today, God bless them, won't just put up with being told "just do it." They want and deserve to be treated with respect, love and patience and dealt with honestly. This book is dedicated to our finding new ways to live with one another especially as parents and children.

I wrote this book for all the people I have worked with who have been harmed in so many ways by Pathological Christianity even when no harm was intended. I dedicate it to the hard-working pastors, teachers, psychotherapists, parents and believers who really do attempt to express respect and compassion and love for others based on a deeply spiritual core which they draw from their convictions, and who want nothing more than for humans to live and breathe and have their being in freedom and choice

Pathological Christianity was written for those who feel trapped in the dark and chilly traps of fundamentalism and feel ashamed of themselves for simply being human, for nothing they ever actually did wrong. It was written for women and men who are searching for a path out of the cold dark world of fundamentalism that so often shows itself as a cheery and grinning self-righteous ideology; for those men and women who can no longer smile and be cheery because they have discovered that their souls were stolen from them by the idealization of people and things and by their giving up their own individual freedoms of thought, feeling and behavior to dogma. I wrote it for children now being trained in the dogmas of self-denigration, chained in the cellars of fear of other religions, cultures and races, and conditioned to see God as a malicious, jealous and mean-spirited patriarch who must have his own selfish way regardless of the cost.

I wrote for those Christian women who have gotten sick and tired of waiting for self-righteous, egotistical and stonewalling men to "go right and see the light" as a result of their prayers, who have finally taken a personal stand in divorce or separation despite the scorn they receive from other so-called "Christians." I wrote for women who have had abortions or been abused or suffered other traumas in life and then had hatred, rejection and exile piled on their person in addition to the wounds they have already suffered.

Also I write for men trapped in the negative patriarchal assumptions that underlie today's American Pathological Christianity. These men inherit the isolation, separation and loneliness of being male in Christian America. They suffer from the demands of being mechanical, aloof and cut off from their psyche and the wellsprings of their life and soul. It is a cold, violent and lonely job to live the role of the American Hero.

There are better ways to live for all of us--men, women and children.

Beware Reader. I speak frankly, sometimes abrasively, in this book. I do not do so merely to provoke, but in the spirit of looking honestly at assumptions and superstitions and delusions that are woven in the cloth of Christianity, or at least in the perversion and abuses I call Pathological Christianity.

Chapter 2. **Christians and "Christians"**

ALL FUNDAMENTALISMS HAVE TWO GOALS. First, to make their leaders rich and powerful in every way possible. Second, to manage all followers in ways that keep them docile, productive of wealth for the leaders, and afraid to act independently. The current American Evangelical Fundamentalist Christian movement is no exception. It is a large, intelligently marketed, wide based action, using the power of expensive, high quality public relations and advertisement, political savvy, psychological theory, political science, business management and sports to build a strong world-wide base. Its goal is to control every single thought, feeling and behavior of every person on earth, and to own and command all the territory on earth.

Fundamentalism of any kind has a tremendous, seductive appeal. Every human being has a deep yearning to belong, to be certain, to be loved and to be powerful. Claim to meet these yearnings and you have found the keys to success of every advertising campaign that has ever been launched, whether for a business, a religious or political movement, a theory of human psychology or any human activity seeking acceptance, advantage, domination.

In some ways it is understandable and even commendable that fundamentalist movements emerge. They naturally evolve to meet our longing for certainty, power and belonging. The trouble is that as a fundamentalism emerges, vigorously greedy individuals inevitably find a way to shrink the number of people who directly benefit from the acquisition of power, money and status, until only a few are the direct recipients of vast amounts of benefits. The certainty of the privileged few in a fundamentalist movement rests on the good will and trance-induced acceptance of the followers. This is exactly what has happened with evangelical fundamentalist Christianity.

I will show you many of the ways that leaders of the evangelical movement have made vast fortunes for themselves-- of course for the "glory of God,"--and how they have accumulated personal control over the way their followers think, believe, feel and act. These leaders even control the most intimate details of their followers' lives in ways often no different to those groups we call *cults*. I will show you how this has happened, why it happened, and precisely how and why to combat these influences.

Fundamentalisms require the sacrifice of countless individual souls for the benefit and exaltation of select few. The *inner sanctum* of the evangelical movement feeds on the guts and hearts of many thousands of victims of the cause.

What do I mean by *pathological Christianity?* Is there such a thing as *healthy Christianity?* Pathological Christianity is the use of the Bible as a tool of domination and supremacy in politics and economics.   Pathological Christianity is the systematic, studied and conscious use of contrivances named *God, Jesus, The Bible and The Family* (not to be confused with any *actually existing* entities carrying such names) for psychological warfare, bigotry, stereotyping, economic and political gain. Pathological Christianity is the hatred of literacy, tolerance, ambiguity and aestheticism, and terror of critical feeling and critical thinking; it is hatred of the natural world *as we find it.*

Pathological Christianity loathes individual freedom and cannot abide psychological depth, symbolic thinking or individual resistance or self-assuredness.   It is greedy, stingy, militaristic, cold and shrewd. Pathological Christianity invents the Jesus it needs at any given moment.   It hates any discussion of history which might displace its *total domination, total control, absolute rule over the minds, hearts and bodies of every living being.*

Make no mistake about it, pathological Christianity is without the slightest shred of doubt the most enormous and influential cult in the United States. The *only* reason why evangelical fundamentalist Christians do not have an absolute monopoly on political and economic power in the United States is because the various leaders of the vast congregations of America have not come to a real coalition. However, this coalition is fast approaching. Any figures I can give you about the numbers of evangelicals, their cadre of political activists or sympathizers at the date of this writing will have been hopelessly subsumed and multiplied by the time you read them.

Every form of training we have in the United States, from schooling to churching to advertising to professional training has the unrelenting goal of pathological conformity, of uniform stupidity among its consumers, of a dulled-out, standardized, timid mind, timid heart and timid soul. I discuss these forms of training and how they operate.

I describe how schools deliberately produce stupidity as part of their Christian heritage, and I will describe numerous things in great detail that individuals can do--if there are any individuals left--to erode the *stupidification* of their kids and themselves in these various institutions of "learning." I will teach you how to erode and disrupt the systematic elimination of individuality that Pathological Christianity aspires to achieve.

The dissenting individual is the most powerful, unstoppable defense against fundamentalism. In fact, the dissenting individual is the *only* weapon that exists as a tool for change of any kind, whether in governments, families, intimate relationships or any other human agency. One extremely courageous and intelligent person can *vastly* erode an entire fundamentalist organization, no matter how huge and systematic its network is.

I have written this book for one reader, whose name I do not know. That reader has an absolutely intimate understanding and knowledge of the workings of a large fundamentalist organization, and he or she has become profoundly disenchanted with that organization and has just recently *seen through* the charade of nobility, service, "spirituality" and all the other words that fundamentalisms use to charm their followers She has recognized that this grand club is really just another political business group with the usual program of greed 'n feed, and feels very betrayed. She was convinced that this gang was indeed different, and now her disillusions are quite real. Suddenly, she gets her sense of humor and irreverence and love of game back, and decides to play. Perhaps she reads this book, gets the basic tricks and uses them to *erode* the structure of the organization. She retains her diplomatic aplomb, and is astonished when things in the structure start falling apart. She thoroughly enjoys herself.

Recovery from fundamentalism? Not in groups! There will be no recovery groups for fundamentalism, since recovery groups are a form of fundamentalism. The only cure and answer to mob psychology is individual psychology, individual maturity, irreverence, humor and *refusal to participate.*

One fundamentalist minister admitting that what is called *faith* in Pathological Christianity is really just timid ignorance could suddenly propel literally thousands of people into a terrifying state of *thought*. Everyone knows we simply cannot have this, because when citizens think, they get unruly.

The Seduction of Fundamentalism is

- *belonging*
- *feeling accepted*
- *having power over other people*
- *a feeling of superiority over others*
- *giving over the hard work of thinking to someone else*
- *feeling that finally you have a perfect parent*
- *believing that finally something will make your life meaningful*
- *a belief that you have somehow transcended your ordinary life*

every one of these seductions will cost you
money
your personal maturity
your confidence and personal integrity

Professional Religion, the *retailing of God*

Nobody really knows whether humans get religious or "spiritual" thoughts and feelings from fear, because we are "receptors" to divine transmissions or simply out of boredom, but most of us do get these thoughts and feelings. Some people only feel "spiritual" glimmerings at the sight of the Grand Canyon, on a clear, starry night, under the influence of lsd or at the threat of imminent death, but then again most people don't think or feel with any depth without a push, a threat or some overwhelming circumstances, spectacles or disasters.   Other people "think deep" all the time, so they never make time to get to the Grand Canyon. A third group, which we will talk about soon, do something we can call *Professional Religion*, and seem to have a penchant for incorporating, politicking and marketing these throbbings of "spirituality."

It is not for lack of speculation that we have no answer to why religions arise. Ask one person you meet why people create religions and he may very well give you an absolutely definitive answer which undoubtedly won't satisfy you. About all we can say is that so many people through time have shown the stubborn tendency to "do religion" that it appears to be something approaching a natural function.

If Og and Magog worship a rock or McGog a war goddess or Mbembe a tiger spirit or McGregor the Papa of a desert Messiah, what does it matter? Each feels he worships the ultimate in some way, and who can doubt it? What about the woman who worships the sex instinct and lays herself down as priestess of the church of Sex? Now hold on, there, partner, let's not go too far!

We are compelled to distinguish between *natural religion* and *professional religion*. Natural religion is this arbitrarily defined urge to make something of it. Whatever the reasons, we see that people apparently are often dissatisfied to just exist and move through life--they seem to feel compelled to make something of it. Og and Magog are very impressed by rocks, not just the little ones they can skip out across the water-- these are minor beings--but the really big ones that a hundred guys couldn't budge. They get together with a few other guys and exchange adjectives about a particular rock: the Glorious Rock, the Magnificent Rock, the Ancient Rock.

This is the *creative phase* of religion. It is all good, clean fun and everybody has a fine time drumming up terrific ways to look at the big rock, under the moon, at the heat of day, during a thunderstorm.   This is the Rock of Ages, here from the beginning, here till the end.   Some clever character scratches and draws on the stone in the moonlight (it turns out to be Magog), and everybody gasps at his heresy for a few days, but then even Og takes up making pictures, and has a swell time doing so. Pretty soon Og and Magog have covered one side of the rock and are enjoying their artwork when some guy from another gang over the hill shows up and says he and his boys have a rock twice as big and with much grander pictures on it in four colors, painted on by his ancestors since way before the moon existed, and Og and Magog are just amateurs.   Well, our boys get hopping mad at the guy from over the hill and whomp him over the head with a nearby branch and declare to the Rock of Ages that they will defend its purity and beauty till their last breath. They have invented Professional Religion.

Professional Religion (PR) is born at the moment when any belief, conviction, creed, doctrine or persuasion a)is no longer playful but is now serious; b) requires money to exist; c)excludes some people and includes others for any reason whatsoever; d)holds that membership in its club is superior to membership in another club.

Professional Religion is a retail business, which sells belonging, faith, afterlife, religious architecture, pardons for ill-doing and the like. Evangelical Christianity sells Jesus and "The Bible" (as opposed to *The Bible*, which is a book).

PR has achieved a kind of success that every insurance man on the planet should envy and strive for, since it sells at sky-high prices---*nothing*.   Unlike insurance, no claims in PR are ever settled to the financial deficit of the Company.

In fact, natural calamities, disasters, accidents, profound illness, death, dismemberment, fire, collision, loss, theft, murder and comas are stimuli for PR to make *more* money, not less, since these events are good reminders of our human limits. Evangelists often use these events to motivate us to join the club, since without the proper (paid) membership in the club, if any of these events were to happen to you, you would not be rocked in the bosom of God but thrown into the pit of Hell. So Join Now.

Professional Religion has never had to pay on a claim or get called up on malpractice regarding its primary products, since it insures nothing at all in this world. The holders of the policy and the beneficiaries (the same) are dead when they might collect and therefore, if PR's claims are false, the clients can never sue, unless perhaps some true Superior Judge holds court in the antechambers of the Celestial Power.

PR has been, is, and will be the most perfect, unassailable, tidy scam going. This is why it attracts some of our most flamboyant sociopaths: these guys and gals know a neat deal when they see one. Americans apparently never learn, because our movies, books, TV have often portrayed the smiling, conniving sociopathic evangelist. It is a kind of *sine qua non* part for American leading men to play at some time in their acting career. As examples, Burt Lancaster played "Elmer Gantry", Robert Mitchum starred in "Night of the Hunter," Steve Martin in "Leap of Faith."

These films and the many exposes about religious leaders flooding the airwaves in recent years have shown that PR is pure profit for the leaders, since there is no product nor service delivered at all except grins, threats, shim-shammery and the Fear-Guilt Lifetime Guarantee. Whatever flows to the collection plate goes to the good pockets of the Lord's Rep.

Our government provides ways for these sly *corporations* to pay no taxes whatsoever, and evangelists with keen lawyers live in mansions tax-free. Of course they portray themselves as humble men with no personal wealth, since everything they own "belongs to the non-profit organization, to the people I serve and to the Lord." If you would like to test whether your local non-profit evangelist indeed feels no ownership of his possessions, go try to take them away from him and see what happens. It is impossible to get accurate figures of the take of the Christian conglomerates, since there is no bite to the laws that require non-profits to make their figures public. Try to get accounting information from any of the several Christian organizations in Colorado Springs. They will most likely give you some figure or no answer at all. If you get some kind of figure, then go take a look at the buildings they are housed in and the staff. Compare the figures with what you see, and then tell me if they can operate on the budget they report. Tax-free.

Professional Religion is not a new thing, of course, but the oldest swindle in the world. The Reformation of the 16th century was an attempt to confront and correct the abuses of power and money by the Catholic Church, but somehow despite the challenges made by Martin Luther and his adherents, the abuses of power just got a wider sales territory and more salesmen. The goal of all fundamentalism is to make its leaders rich and powerful in every way possible, while demanding allegiance, sacrifice, assent and loyalty from its followers.

Please let me repeat that. *The goal of all fundamentalism is to make its leaders rich and powerful in every way possible, while demanding allegiance, sacrifice, assent and loyalty from its followers.* To this end, all leaders in Professional Religion must be fundamentalists and never truly open-minded. Open-mindedness is not profitable, powerful, nor territorial, and PR cannot tolerate this. The goal of PR is closed membership, the advertising campaign dedicated to making followers (read *contributors*) believe they are in possession of a treasure and that they are unique, superior and shrewd. They bought their stock at ten dollars a share and are going to sell it for a million per share...in heaven. That is, as long as they follow the straight and narrow path, the "way of Jesus and the *Bible*". It is possible to fall down, but Jesus will lift you up, *if and only if...* These "ifs" are discussed in the chapter "The ABC's of Pathological Christian Psychology."

Spirituality

.Within the realm of Pathological Christianity, and whose influence extends into the realm of almost everything we know today, the word *spirituality* has the following meaning, which definition I will use in the rest of this chapter and beyond:

Spirituality means controlling your sexual urges. It means smiling and not feeling conflict. It means that you can conquer bad habits, and that their seductions do not have power over you. It means that you float above chaos into a settled, measured peace with Jesus. It means that no matter what happens to you or those you love, you recognize it is God's Will--and that he wishes it to happen or it would not have happened: this is called "grace." Spirituality is something you can get, a state you can attain through certain actions and mental training, particularly prayer; not just any prayer, but "Christian" prayer.

In other word, "spirituality" is a product which can be acquired through the right actions, the right allegiances, the right attitudes. Professional Religion has always tried to portray itself as a unique source for the acquisition of ultimate meaning, value and afterlife privileges. Evangelical Christianity has a sort of "franchise" attitude about the distribution and procurement of its products, Jesus and *The Bible*. Within today's business market, one might be frankly shocked that no one has trademarked such expressions as "accept Jesus Christ as your personal savior." However, clearly only "authorized" franchise Christians, those who lip-synch certain principles, use prescribed words in their vocabulary, put a stick-figure fish in their business advertisement and hold the line on conservative political positions will actually be vested in the Company, that is, the Company of the Lord, on Judgment Day.

For Pathological Christians, "spiritual" translates as politically acceptable. The term has little to do with detachment from worldly matters. The writer and monk Thomas Merton once wrote an essay entitled "Everything That Is, Is Holy." He was portraying the view of the mystic--the model of the "spiritual." His point is that a spiritual perspective accepts everything that is, rejecting nothing at all. This is the exact opposite from what we find in Pathological Christianity, where nearly everything is rejected, scrutinized, sterilized and screened out as the devil's domain, and only certain words, people, attitudes, actions or places on earth viewed as acceptable or *Christian*. The Good Lord made the world, but evil humans corrupted it, so now it is a place of damnation and pain, unless we allow Jesus to heal it for us, or in the places where Jesus inhabits, such as the hearts of His believers.

This is not spirituality nor natural religion but Professional Religion--the business of politics. It is about territory and ownership and the control of the minds and bodies of people. Professional Religion is forever hungry for more land, money and people, and the more it can promote its products and get people to believe that its products are the only ones of value, the more it can re-capitalize, expand, and dominate.

There is an old principle, known to fraternities, clubs and other organizations through time, and borne out by research, that the harder it is to get into a group, the more it costs and the more exclusive it is, the more highly people esteem membership in that group. These principles also promote group cohesion, competition for membership and devotion to the group's purpose, the leaders and the *modus operandi* or methods used to achieve goals.

HOW TO RECOGNIZE FUNDAMENTALIST PROFESSIONAL RELIGION

Professional Religion (by whatever name) includes any or all of these:

- Markets "spirituality": The game is soothing the hurts and getting rich
- Sells Fear, "Bible" and "Jesus. In other situations it might masquerade as "enlightenment," "the sutras" or "the guru." The Greatest Con Game of All.
- Portrays itself as having The One and Only Inside Track on "The Will of God". Hold some claim to having *unique knowledge, unique understanding* or the like.
- Maintains that God speaks to "special people"--those under the sway of its brand of Professional Religion.
- Uses "The Will of God" to control people. Says that it does or thinks or believes something (and you ought to as well) because it is the "Will of God".
- Maintains that there is some "ideal" type of person. In Pathological Christianity, this is the Christian Soldier; whip'em into shape with *The Bible*

- Commands followers to be Obedient because God says so. In other words, refuses real dialogue.
- Claims you must be *loyal* because you are damned if you are not. New Age fundamentalists, for example, claim that you will get *ill* if you are not loyal to some discipline or other.
- Sees individual thinking, private thought or feeling or idiosyncratic imagery as *sin.*
- Has some kind of *installment plan* for your investment in the afterlife. For example, tithing or giving to "ministries" is a kind of "layaway plan" for getting your angel wings later.
- Has a foundation of Bigotry: only "certain people" are saved, therefore, worthy
- Actively seeks new converts. Has some kind of Marketing Plan.
- Has the goal of getting a better and bigger building to meet in.
- Offers a place to hide from conflict in a difficult world, sees itself as a shelter against the "dangerous outside world."
- Sees itself as a compensation for the hurts in the real world

- Offers a method to rationalize or make sense of pain: a balm for suffering
- Has some plan for De-Sexing The Populace: Sex is "dangerous"; substitute with "spirit"
- Offers a vision of "Specialness" and "entitlement"
- Has very little humor about its beliefs.

A Lost Opportunity

Diane is the beloved secretary in the principal's office at JFK High School. She is a delightful, considerate, warm person, known for her cheerfulness and for the fact that she seems to know each one of the twenty-five hundred students and the faculty personally and to take an interest in each and every one of them.. She is one of those people who is far more than an employee, more like a mother and friend to everyone. Despite the fact that she has a few detractors who consider her a "busybody" who tries to stick her nose into everyone's business, parents, students and administration alike fine her the "rock" of the school, almost the essence of the school itself.

Diane has two daughters who attend JFK, who are active and well-liked students with many friends. One night something grievous and shocking happened. A friend of Diane's daughters, Samantha, was beaten and raped after a basketball game. The girl's clothes were taken, and she had to limp her way to a neighborhood house, bloody, in great pain and utterly humiliated.

Two days after the incident, Diane called me and made an appointment for her older daughter, Jean, saying that Jean wanted to talk over some things with me rather than with Gordon Preston, the minister of the church. Then Diane said something I found intriguing. She informed me "not to put any crazy notions in her head." I was fascinated by this comment and asked, "what do you think of as 'crazy notions'?" She said, "well, I just mean make her see things logically--the right way."

Whenever anyone is being "sent" to me for therapy, I suspect that they are being sent in to be "re-tooled" to fit the expectations of someone. I didn't ask Diane what she meant by seeing things "the right way." I assumed, rightly as it turned out, that Jean would tell me what it was that Diane expected.

Jean was very distraught, frightened and angry about what had happened to her friend. But she was actually more dismayed by her mother's reaction to the rape. When Diane heard what had happened, she said, "Poor Samantha, she must feel awful. We must pray for her in her torment. There must have been some hidden sin in her for such a thing to have happened. Even though she is hurting now, God has his reasons. I am just glad you girls are Christians, and that *God has protected you* from this suffering."

Jean had suddenly and overwhelmingly recognized the dark side of her mother and her mother's beliefs. In a flash she understood what one of her boyfriends had said to her during a spat: "Your mother helps a lot of people and does a lot of good stuff, but I can't stand her because she thinks that she is better than anybody else and that no one can do anything right except her, and you are turning out just like her!" At the time of this fight, she thought her boyfriend was just a little brat, but now she saw he was right.

Jean went on, "She thinks that God is punishing Samantha for something and that her daughters are these little godly angels, protected by God just because we go to church and all that. That's just crap! Samantha is actually a much better person than me, she's sweet and kind, and never hurt a flea. Just because she doesn't go to our church, my mother thinks she should be gang raped and shamed like that? I feel like slapping my mother, she's such a bitch!"

I told Jean about her mother's charge to get Jean to "see things the right way." I explained that part of Diane's reaction was most likely a natural mother's response to defend her children, to keep them safe, but warned her that I couldn't speak for Diane. In my view, I continued, this was clearly a moment ripe for the two of them, indeed for the whole family, to work on the questions of personal maturity, healthy disagreements and keeping connections with each other even in conflict. This was of particular importance since Jean, in her senior year, was planning to move to another state for school, and to leave home.

I encouraged Jean to have her own thoughts, opinions and feelings about the rape of her friend, as well as on other subjects, but to keep the emotional connection with her mother (and the left-out person in all of this, her father). The secret to a satisfying experience of leaving home and of adult relationships between family members is the combination of latitude for individual thought and feeling along with a solid, enduring and demonstrated love between family members.

When I told Jean I would speak with her mother about having some family sessions to encourage these experiences, she just snorted at me and said, "my mother will *never* come to any family or any other kind of therapy. She thinks that all she needs to do is to pray and believe and follow the Bible, whatever that means, and if things go wrong, it's not her fault."

Sadly enough, her words came true. I spoke to Diane, suggesting family sessions. She was very courteous and polite, but the essence of her words spoke clearly of her rigid and righteous position. I could see that her daughters--and her husband--would have to struggle and fight for any inch of individuality they could get around her.

When I called, Diane said to me, "Dr. Vogt, I am sure that you are well-meaning, but it is my faith in Christ that has given me and my family every good thing we have today. God entrusted these girls to me, to keep them pure and free from the harm of the world and to keep them for His Service. If you were a true Christian, I am sure you would see that I have to keep these girls on a straight and narrow path since the slightest bad influence can poison a person forever. I don't bear you any hard feelings, but I know that if you come to Christ yourself and devote your expertise to the Lord, you will be a happier man than you are, and will be serving the true source of all good things and our protection. I will be praying for you."

Jean left for college a couple of months ago. I got a call and a letter from her. She had understood very clearly what it was I was suggesting. In her letter, she wrote:

"I am sad knowing that my mother cannot tolerate real closeness or any disagreement from me or anyone else. I now understand why my dad has to act like such a mouse around her. I am angry at both of them, though I love each of them very dearly. I won't give up trying to have a good relationship with my mother and the hope that one day we can talk as adults to each other, but I know I must respect the fact that she probably won't change, at least from what I do or say. All I know is that I am going to keep developing my own thinking and feelings and beliefs, and to try to keep myself open to other people's views. I am so afraid of conflict, and always feel that I'd much rather agree and be quiet than argue with anybody at all. I am so afraid of being *bad*. But I know I am going to have to get over that fear if I am going to be the kind of person I want to be. I am ready for the challenge, and feeling really *excited.*"

I feel confident that *Jean's* children will grow up with the self-assurance that comes from facing the world rather than hiding from it. I only wish that Diane could relax her grip, her need to be right and her fear of being *human*. She could gain so much in the process, including far greater friendship with her own daughter.

godliness, the will of God, and personal power

We saw in Diane and Jean's story how Pathological Christianity tries to demand that children completely give up their capacity to think, feel or act autonomously in order to deserve the title "godly" or "good." It is a sad irony that even kids who try to live up to this mandate to be obedient and mindless, *especially girls*, will still be blamed if something goes wrong in the family. This is ironic since kids are taught to be obedient and powerless but also to take the blame if something goes bad. They are taught to believe that if something goes well, it is because of God; if it turns out badly, it is because of *you*.

Girls in pathological Christian families in particular are taught that they have no real power except to accept Jesus, trust in the Lord and wait for God to provide a man. Something that happens all too often is that a "man of God" sees this as a ripe opportunity for some virgin-harvesting.

So picture a young girl who has been trained all her life to respect authority, in particular where it concerns the church, "godly" people and men in particular. Take into account a culture-wide confusion about sex and love, as well as her desire to please and to be touched, and you have the formula for a little pregnant Christian, impregnated by a "man of God."

And when she begins to swell up, who do you think gets the blame? The preacher? Not likely, though he'll have to look "hang-dog" for a while. No, it will be the girl. Somehow she seduced him, that man of God. So she is simultaneously told that she has no power and blamed if things go bad.

Power is in the hands of the Man of God and indirectly in the grasp of his followers. So what is godliness-power, how do you get it, and how do you know if you have it? First, you must not refer to it as "power" but rather as "godliness," since everything is God's, and only belongs to him. I can't figure out why God might want a Lincoln Town Car to drive around in, but his loyal servant surely does. So the deal is this: you trust in the Lord and accept whatever he gives to you.

And here is what you do. When the moolah rolls in, when you are getting a really high life style, you keep praying. You will know you are perfect and holy and that God has "raised you up" when what you want is what you get. That you will know you are in perfect accord with the will of God. Then you can think, "God would not have given this to me, all this wealth and power, if it weren't what he wanted me to have." If you are poor it is God's will; and if you are rich, it is his plan, for reasons which must remain inscrutable. It is "just God's will."

The message in this is, whatever you get, be grateful, because it is God's will. This is a great deal for those who have the advantage of a pricey education, some family dough or a particular talent or two, an acquaintance or relative who can fork over the bucks to you, or if you escape illness somehow.

It is a little different story if you happen to have been born in the wrong place at the wrong time without a nickel, and surrounded by dangerous influences. But no matter, say the evangels, just remember to be grateful, to show grace in adversity.

There is something to having grace in adversity, resiliency, strength and personal pride regardless of your circumstances, especially if you got a raw deal from the beginning. It seems there is always a grain of truth in the messages of Pathological Christianity, a kernel of value, which gets twisted to the disadvantage of some and to the advantage of others. The message of grateful and gracious acceptance of your circumstance, thinking it is God's will yields the benefit of a feeling of satisfaction--at least temporary contentment in the believer's attitude. There is a kind of wisdom in that, but the irony is that is the kind of advice nearly always given by people who are enjoying the fruits of the earth, those persons well off with prospects unending.

The fact that certain people are wealthy, powerful, influential and such is quite rarely the result of their being a fine and noble person and almost universally because they are ruthless, focused, ambitious, willing to take great risks, and usually perfectly happy to exploit any or everyone in shooting range for their own self-centered ends. Is this what is meant by God's will?

Some sort of reversed logic must apply here, one that says that God is indeed a being who enjoys ruthlessness, ambition and the like, and therefore gives his servants (what, owners of places like K-Mart or big-time commercial real estate brokers?) who demonstrate these qualities the goodies of life. Also apparent in this logic is that God loves men better than women, since men earn far more and get far better jobs on average.

But also Pathological Christianity teaches us to be grateful for emotional hardships, to turn against all that is healthy and natural and normal in ourselves, even to the point of denying a mother's primary instincts, as this example will show.

Darlene Jensen had a beautiful daughter of three years of age named Collette. She and her husband Jim had been married for eight years and had tried and prayed and consulted doctors to have children for the first five years with no success. Then when they had nearly given up hope, Darlene got pregnant, and gave birth to Collette, a healthy, radiant child, who was the joy of both parents' lives, their dream come true. They gave thanks and the glory to Jesus for the presence of Collette in their lives. When Jim and Darlene talked about her, they called her "The Little Miracle."

When Darlene got pregnant, the Jensens moved to a larger house in the same neighborhood they lived in, one with a yard, a little garden spot and two stories, including a good-sized bedroom for Collette and even her own bathroom. Jim and Darlene thought this would be plenty of space for all three of them even when Collette got to her teen years.

One afternoon while Darlene was vacuuming the house, Collette lost her footing on the staircase and plunged down to the landing below, knocking her head on the oak flooring. When Darlene found her, Collette was bleeding from the mouth, nose and ears and convulsing on the floor. Darlene stood numb and in total disbelief for a moment, as if she were witnessing something unreal or in a movie. Then in a flash it all came into focus what had happened. She called an ambulance.

Collette was in a coma for three weeks and then died. She never regained consciousness.

I got involved when Jim called me for an appointment about two months after the death of his daughter. He was shaking and moving in and out of sobbing from the moment he entered my office. I saw so much pain in this man that I imagined holding him and rocking him like a baby until he felt better, which of course I did not do, but tried to do through my voice and acceptance of him in his suffering.

When I asked him what brought him to me, he talked at first of the fact that the death of his child had rendered him almost incompetent at work, kept him up nearly every night, brought him to question everything in his life. He said that his spiritual life was intact, that he did not hold God or anyone else responsible for what had happened, which he had at first, but rather that now he felt he just had a sadness that would never end and he questioned whether he would ever be able to function at work or any other part of his life again.

I assured Jim that his reactions were perfectly normal, that indeed he would never get over some deep current of sadness and longing to have his daughter with him, but that he would indeed be able to function and regain his competence and even feel happiness again in his life. I congratulated him for deciding to talk with a therapist, which many men will not do, and then asked him how his wife Darlene was doing.

He gave me an odd, piercing look, and then said, "My wife? She's got it all worked out--that's just it. I am going off my rocker here and she's walking around like nothing happened."

At my suggestion, Darlene came in with Jim for the next appointment. She said that she'd "do anything" to help Jim along to getting the same kind of feeling of "joyful feeling of grace" she had. I asked her to explain. She told me her story:

"I saw Collette there at the bottom of the stairs, bleeding and jerking around and begged God for it not to be true. For the first couple of days while she was in her coma, I was angry, indignant, couldn't sleep, I was like Jim is now, poor guy. But then one morning I woke up and remembered what we Christians are taught, and that is to be grateful for all things, knowing that God has a plan. Our job is to accept the beauty in it and try to see it, because all is from God and we owe the creator and his son Jesus infinite gratitude for the creation of the world and for our salvation. God took my child to Himself, and I am deeply grateful to Him for taking my baby to His side and out of this world. It is a joyous thing and I praise God for it."

Perhaps Darlene was doing the only thing she could, fending off the staggering agony that a loving mother naturally feels when a precious child dies. Perhaps she was using the only tool to endure against the storm of feeling she feared might come up if she "gave in" to her emotions. Anyone can respect the need for some defense against these feelings. In addition, there is great value in her surrender to the fact of the death of her daughter, and her intense need to find some kind of meaning in the death rather than to sink into a debilitating and decompensating state of mourning. It is good to keep moving even in the darkest hours of grief, even if at a greatly reduced pace. Jim had almost dropped out of reach, partly because there was no one at home with whom he could share his grief. Darlene was inaccessible, unreachable, righteous.

Many things troubled me about her answer. One was that she had moved to a rigid and uncompromising and superior conclusion extremely quickly. She had not even allowed herself to be *conscious* of what had happened, and of the depth of her sadness, but had banished and deflected her pain by using the shield of "Christian" formulas. She had truly exiled all real maternal feelings and replaced them with words and ideas, shutting herself off from the healing power of staying with, enduring and coming out on the other side of suffering. She was faking herself out.

Several clues told me that she was not so "resolved" about this as she pretended to be. Jim told me that Darlene could not hear of any stories about children in pain, or of "happy families." Darlene had thrown away all of Collette's things right after she died. Jim told me that she hardly left the house anymore except to go to church, where she went almost every day; she had not shown up for work at her part-time job for two weeks; she did not speak to the neighbors.

Darlene smiled and appeared unruffled by all this talk. She spoke to Jim in a condescending voice, "Well, Jim, to me it looks like you are the one who is falling apart, if anyone is in this family." Darlene's "belief system" had resulted in another great casualty--she had cut herself off almost entirely from any intimacy with Jim. I suspect she could not "afford it," since if she felt tender emotions with her husband, she might have to recognize and contend with many other strong feelings, so she would not risk opening herself with him.

As a result of her actions, under the guidance of her evangelical pastor, Darlene had chosen a way of responding that denied her the profound experience of sharing the intimacy of grief with Jim, and the deep integration that can come with facing one's own pain head on, enduring it with integrity and bravery, and letting the natural course of meaning that self-examination can provide. She had shucked all of this for a set of formulas that isolated her, made her chilly and aloof and would cost her the rest of her life. Somehow I doubt that such choices are what Jesus had in mind.

I tried to intervene with her for her own and Jim's sake, but to no avail. She was dug in. Jim continued to work with me. I taught him how to move through his grief, how to keep himself from spiraling into depression, and referred him to a men's group, where he felt quite accepted by other men, to his amazement. But as it became clearer to him that Darlene was steadfastly refusing to attend to her own feelings or to let him get closer to her, Jim began to fear he would want to divorce her. Divorce for any reason was out of the question in Jim's "Christian" beliefs, so he chose to discontinue his therapy with me. He stated that self-awareness was becoming too great a risk for him, and felt that he had strayed too far from the evangelical teachings he and Darlene had practiced for years.

In our last session, Jim told me that Darlene was "overjoyed" that he was stopping his therapy, since she considered it a threat to their marriage, and that he was "coming back to the Lord." I told Jim I was afraid for him, and he told me he had no idea what I was talking about. He had already stepped back into the unconsciousness that Pathological Christianity requires. A great opportunity for Jim and Darlene to go deeply into the intimacy that they could have experienced after the death of their daughter was missed.

I saw Jim in the grocery store a month after our last session. He looked haunted and afraid, a zombie. He actually looked worse than when I had first seen him; at least then, he seemed alive, even though in great suffering. His eyes seemed to be receding into his face, and were dark and gray. He hardly recognized me when he saw me, though we had worked together weekly for several months. I asked him how he was, and he told me that he was "fine, just fine." I felt a chill in my spine as I walked away from him.

the *will of god*: a fantasy of male domination

The phrase "will of God" can be used to justify all kinds of bad behavior, from child abuse to wars to environmental devastation. Recognition in our lives of the "will of God" is a pure anthropomorphism, a belief that God must be just like us psychologically, but he can be excused bad moods, harmful acts, neglect, self-centeredness, domination or pouting, because he is more powerful, controls things, is more intelligent, is responsible for our being here, grants us the privilege of life, and has been around longer than us.

So, extrapolating from this, if you are smarter, more powerful, make things happen and have been around in power a long time, you too get to play god, know a little of what god is like, speak for the god, and generally get to have the same excuses that the deity does, that is, bad moods, harmful acts, unconsciousness, domination of others, pouting, etc. This describes exactly the fantasy that many men would like to have fulfilled, to be unchallenged, supreme, served, the center of all good things. What better way to get the privileges of the god than to portray him in your own image, and then offer yourself as his humble servant, trying to *do his will?*

When we say of a person (and this term is often applied to girl children) that *she is willful,* we mean that she wants things to go a certain way, that is, *her* way, and that there is no other way she will accept, that she will campaign in any way necessary to get her way, whether by refusal to act or direct act.

I remember trying to get my four year old daughter to eat sweet peas. She didn't like them and wouldn't eat them. I made her sit at the table for a long time, until she would eat them. She never did, since I relented after a couple of hours. I remember feeling that I wanted to slug her, but recognizing she was certainly the one in power. Many fathers do not give in when such power struggles happen, and some force-feed their kids (whether food or other substances or beliefs, etc.) They are attempting to break their children, like one "breaks" horses, of their will, of their autonomy, and force them to conform.

One can always hold a god up to justify actions, and many fundamentalists are trained today to use corporal or other punishment to drive their children like cattle into conformity through fear. The evangelical holds up some smoke and mirror justification in *Bible* or *Christian Family Life* or some other rhetoric, as a shield against thinking and self-reflection and breadth of understanding, founding their self-centered behavior in some arbitrary fantasy called *the will of god.*

*The expression **the will of God** is the final refuge of the*

*egotist; the purpose of the
evoking the expression is to
justify self-centeredness and to
shield oneself against the hard
work of mature thinking and
feeling.*

Evangelicals and all other religious fundamentalists portray their god as zealous, paranoid, territorial, autocratic, self-centered, demanding thoughtless conformity. They excuse him for being rigid and unmoving in his demands, expectations and meted out punishments. The reason for this is that the fundamentalist can only get power and control through a tool which requires silent acquiescence and conformity. The best tool going is to use the expression *the will of God.*

The Largest Cult in America: Pathological Christianity

what is a "cult"?

- A "cult" is any group which professes (without laughing at itself) to have the one and only and true answer and cure for human suffering and search for meaning--a cure only available through membership and obedience to its rules for proper thought, feeling and behavior. Further, the group got its calling from a *higher authority* of some kind, which usually offers some really neat reward for total compliance, such as *heaven*, and some really horrible punishment for transgression, such as *hell.*

- There are leaders who "know what is right," who have "special powers" or "special gifts" and therefore deserve the attention and respect of the followers.

Pathological Christianity, whether it is in the guise of Evangelical Christianity or some other group, is the procedure of creating **cults**

All **cults** have the same Closed System structure.

1. They are hostile to and feel themselves superior over outside influences (because *those people and those ideas* can "hurt" or destroy cult members).

2. They guard their own turf. Leaders invent and keep their agendas, territory and goals like pit bulls. A favorite trick in Pathological Christianity is "it's God's Will." Woe to he who questions.

3. Cults emotionally and intellectually tyrannize their followers. What you feel and think is always under scrutiny -- will it pass through the "eye of the needle"?

4. Cults usurp the world of the followers. They drain followers of their energy, their financial resources and their meaning. They do not allow dialogues or open discussion or individuality. Anything individual is dangerous and a threat to group cohesion.

Chapter 3: **The ABC's of Pathological Christian Psychology**

A. Pathological Christian Counselors: Ethical Abuse
B. Binds and Paradoxes
C. "Right" and "Wrong": "Godly" and "Ungodly"
D. The Jekyll and Hyde Syndrome
E. Abuse of Psychological Data
F. Pathological Conditioning
G. Christian Psychology

A: Pathological Christian Counselors: Ethical Abuses

WHILE IT HAS BECOME INCREASINGLY CLEAR that a proper and thoroughgoing psychotherapy needs to include at the minimum a respect for spiritual dimensions of human life, at the same time it has happened that many psychotherapists have simply substituted the dogma of their own personal beliefs for high quality psychotherapy. They have practiced a brand of personal doctrinism in lieu of a psychotherapeutic approach to help their clients discover spirituality within themselves. To substitute one dogmatism, (that is the dogmatism that arises from ignorance about one's own character, one's own family patterns, about interpersonal relationships) for another one (such as that human beings are really "love seeking light forms" or some other arbitrary conclusion) has not accomplished a proper goal of psychotherapy. Nor is it appropriate to psychotherapy to ever align itself to any religious tradition. This is a misuse of the patient's trust. It is not our goal as psychotherapists ever to teach the basic rules of life or understanding. Our true goal is to help our clients discover for themselves what is useful, meaningful to their own psyches.

So-called Christian counseling is really nothing more than politics, the use of doctrines in attempts to convert. It is conquering the savages--missionary work, not psychotherapy in any sense of the world. An examination of what passes for

Christian psychology or counseling will reveal to any thinking person that what is really being practices is a form of "Ozark Politics," a "believe it or else" approach which disregards and even abhors the individual psyche. For the Christian counselor to say *individual psyche* is the same as saying *witchcraft* or *sin*. If you don't believe me, just ask the next evangelical you meet.

If these were really *Christian* counselors, they would be practicing a form of love and acceptance. That is certainly not what one finds. Dogma, herding, and absolutism are the order of the day.

One problem with identifying damaging absolutism, the kind that insidiously robs the soul, is that the majority of the new evangelists don't look stupid or obvious like their predecessors. They often do not dress in glittering white suits, sport pompadour hair styles, speak in shrill Tennessee tones, or even rant and rave. They have discovered the power of *advertising*. They have learned to sound like *caring professionals*. They appear *assimilated* and portray themselves as normal citizens who are living, thinking and feeling the way any normal human being should.

Evangelists have learned to shed the imagery of *difference* in Christians and instead have adopted the stance of *normalcy*. In the early, formative time of Christianity, Christians were different than the Jews and the Greek and Roman polytheists who surrounded and controlled the definition of "normalcy." In those times, it was the infant religion Christianity and its followers who were "weird," and out of the ordinary run of the world.

Much was made of this position of underdog, scapegoat and victim. The Christians were "thrown to the lions," and indeed were made to suffer in their day for their beliefs They developed a psychology of entitlement as payment for their distress. Since they sincerely believed that their budding religion was the true and only salvation for all humankind and that they had been given the charge to convert and dominate, they viewed themselves as entitled and destined to eventually rule the world. The psychology of oppressed people teaches that frequently they view themselves as far superior to their oppressors, partly because of the strength they have developed under the regimen of persecution. *One day they will rise up* and overthrow and the world will be far better in their hands. However, it never is, because oppressed people bear a seed of resentment and revenge, and at the first chance, act it out on others when they get power.

The image of Christ is that of one humiliated, misunderstood, tormented, arbitrarily punished, beaten and murdered, yet one who is victorious after all by conquering death and arising to lead the oppressed out of darkness and into triumph and ascendancy. He tricks his malefactors by exercising a far superior form of control and domination--that over life and death itself, and sin and salvation and the rest.

The Winking Jesus

I once saw a piece of plastic trickery art , a picture of Jesus. If you looked at the image from one side, you saw Jesus suffering on the cross, bloody, gnarled, twisted upon himself in pain and suffocation. If you looked from the other side, you saw him grinning and winking at you, in the standard facial gesture of "get it?" Although crude and stingy, certainly not generous in intent, this representation did demonstrate some basic deceit in the Christian scheme, to portray oneself as suffering and victimized while dominating and controlling the whole drama.

Christians have done this for a long time, and for very cagey reasons. It is an exquisite strategy which allows you to " have your cake and eat it too."

By portraying yourself as poor, downtrodden and misunderstood, you demand sympathy, consideration and kindness. Others have no right to attack or malign you, just as *those people* had no right to attack or malign Jesus. You have your power and superiority, carte blanche to rule and control the world, because *God wants you to.* You have proof in Christ, in the Bible and in the clear rightness of riches and might that have accumulated in the "Christian nations" the last several centuries.

Even today, with the fundamental doctrines, tenets and principles of Christianism permeating every single aspect of Western thought, belief, business, relationships, families, philosophy and views of self, world and afterlife, there are evangelists complaining that Christianity doesn't get enough attention, that Christians are mocked or that the "Christian way of life" is viewed with disdain. It is extraordinary that with nearly two thousand years of Christian domination of the world with all the ensuing terror, destruction and despotism that has arisen as a direct result of Christianity these evangels are still whining for us to give Christianity "another chance." It is tempting to say that Christianity itself (or Pathological Christianity, which is the same thing, since the pathology is inescapable) is the problem. This is because Pathological Christianity is a religion of blame and scapegoating. It is a developmentally immature position about the world, correlating with a stage of psychological development in the individual that demands black and white thinking, single-minded results, rules and control of thought, feeling and behavior. Pathological Christianity is a religion meant to control young children, to socialize an immature creature. Pathological Christianity is not a way of life that encourages, promotes or even allows maturity in the individual. It is a politic of social control.

The psychology of Pathological Christianity is the psychology of business, advertising and political power, and the counselor or therapist who uses the modifier "Christian" is an agent of a regime. If evangelical Christianity were a message of love and tolerance, there would never be a need for the modifier "Christian" before the term therapist or any other word, because the love and tolerance would come from an acceptance of human diversity. However, Pathological Christianity, or in this case, Pathological Christian Counseling, is an act of domination and usurping. It is an act of *colonization*.

Is it too strong to use the word *colonization* to describe the activities of Pathological Christianity? Not at all, since the clear goal is to bring people "under the flag" of evangelical fundamentalism; the overstated goal of this colonization is *total and unquestioning conformity* to the world view, rules, ways of thought feeling and behavior outlined by the evangelical crusade.

It is never appropriate for psychotherapy to align itself to any religious tradition. This is a misuse of the patient's trust. It is not our goal as psychotherapists ever to teach the basic rules of life or understanding. Our true goal is to help our clients discover for themselves what is useful and meaningful to their own psyches. Our job is to help each patient become him or herself, not to mirror our own misgivings, insecurities, political persuasions or even "spiritual paths."

Recently, a female colleague of mine, Teresa, had a conversation in a restaurant with a well-known "Christian psychologist," whom I will call "James." She was new to the area and wanted to discuss developing her client base. She had been on friendly terms with evangelicals in her former locale, though her own beliefs had changed recently. Though still committed to many basic Christian views, she was "in recovery" from Pathological Christianity.

Teresa had recently gotten a divorce from a minister known to and respected by James. Her former husband was a charmer who had been living a high life on donations to a "ministry" he had founded to help drug addicts, though almost the entirety of the donations went into his own pocket. He himself was an unrepentant drug addict and alcoholic who slept away his days and literally had no interactions with his wife or two daughters for ten years. He had countless affairs and Teresa had always taken him back, forgiving him and praying, playing "good Christian woman." Finally she had enough and had divorced him.

James knew enough of the story to recognize the pattern of mistreatment and refusal to change that comes with substance abuse and a lifetime of disregarding personal health and attention to responsibility for oneself. Even Christian psychologists get enough "secular" training to recognize personal irresponsibility, and this "minister" was certain a ripe case.

Yet when Teresa spoke with James about building her practice, she got a lesson in the rigidity of Pathological Christianity that she should have expected, yet hoped that she would not hear again.

The two of them spoke about their views of therapy, the curative or healing process, what is called "theoretical orientation." James asked Teresa, "What is your position on divorce, and on clients getting divorced?"

Teresa answered, "I believe it is up to each person to make up his or her mind about what is best for him or her. I support my clients to do their own thinking and feeling and to choose their own course of action."

James's face tightened. He paused and then spoke. "That's not the kind of counseling *I* do. I believe in the *two-pillar* view of divorce that is Biblical. Divorce is not acceptable, and divorce is *adultery*. People must know that they go against the will of God when they divorce, and that divorce is unacceptable in the eyes of the Lord. I tell my clients what is *right*."

Despite her experience with this kind of rhetoric, Teresa still found herself shocked. "Are you God, that you know exactly what is right for every human being?"

"No," answered James in a slow, controlled, patronizing voice that showed he was prepared for this question and ready to lead yet another sinner toward the Lord if she were only willing. "I am not God, but I do have the word and covenant with God through Jesus and the Bible, and these sources tell me precisely what is good and right and just in God's eyes. Divorce is wrong, and I am simply transmitting this message to my clients, who will thank me when they experience the grace of God in their lives by attending to their duty and following his will."

Teresa looked at James and thought in her mind, *you arrogant, self-righteous little worm, how dare you play Savior.* She wanted to yell at him or defend all women who were being squelched down by such a system into the acceptance of abuse, many of them far worse than what she had experienced, by such a male-dominated fantasy of woman as "helpmate." Then she asked, ready for the pat answer she knew would come, "And what was I to do with my ex-husband?"

"You should have stayed married, prayed, sought counsel, followed the will and love of Jesus rather than departing from his Path" James moderated his voice, spoke softly and with a little affected tremor in his throat. "Perhaps you are ready to pray with me now."

"Can you possibly be serious? Do you have any idea at all how insulting and vicious you are being with me at this moment?"

James hung his head, his arms on the back of the bench where he was sitting, making his little restaurant-booth Cross. He was ready to go on the Cross for this fallen sister, but she obviously was not ready to come back to Jesus. "You see, Teresa, why I cannot refer clients to you? You have fallen from the Path. You do not believe the *two-pillar* view of divorce from our Lord. You will take your clients to *unrighteousness.* I could not allow you to do this, of course. The married soul is one soul. When people divorce, they destroy what God wants. I cannot support you going against My Lord. We cannot let our personal will interfere with that of God. This is mere selfishness"

Teresa felt, if only temporarily, many of the old feelings so familiar to her during her days with her ex-husband, when she was trying to be the "perfect Christian woman." She briefly felt terrorized and afraid for her soul--what if James was right about what he was saying? What if she indeed was being selfish? She was awash with guilt and self-hatred, and seeking repentance not only for what she had done, but for her *very being.*

Then she reflected on her time with her ex-husband, and the twenty years she had devoted to becoming a "good Christian." She was flooded with examples of maneuvers used by her husband and so many other men and women in the "movement" to squelch individual thinking and feeling. So many personal fears, insecurities and *intellectual laziness and cowardice* of evangels were covered and laid to rest by merely subsuming and maintaining the status quo through incantations of the words *Jesus, Bible, sin, will of God.*

Teresa regained her composure. She looked James in the eyes and came back to her present self, a confident, competent, mature adult, with insecurities and some uncertainties of course, because these are part of the realism of maturity. At the moment, she was aware primarily of the strength that comes from moving into maturity and away from the shelter and hiding behind the formulas of fundamentalism.

James could not tolerate her look. It challenged all he was afraid of--personal maturity, natural wisdom, psychological competence. He looked away and then tried to force himself to look at her again, and soon muttered, "I have to leave. I have an appointment soon."

"No," said Teresa. "Sit down. You have had your say. I allowed you to talk, and now I am going to talk and you are going to listen."

James arose and started to leave. " I have to see clients now," he said. "I will pray for you, that you can see the way of Jesus."

Teresa laughed. "I see you are leaving the bill for me to pay. Doesn't that strike you as symbolic?" James tried to take the bill, but Teresa snatched it away. "No, mister, you can't get off that easy. My soul is not for sale, like yours is."

"I have no idea what you are talking about," snorted James.

"I am sure you know exactly what I am talking about," grinned Teresa. "You are not half as stupid as you are trying to appear. Hadn't you better go inoculate your clients against people like me? Run along now."

James glowered at Teresa and then spun and strode out of the restaurant.

Teresa is a rare example of one who has thoughtfully, purposely and carefully disentangled herself from the cult-like influence of Pathological Christianity. Her hard work has helped her recognize the self-protective, self-insulating purpose of the principles held by fundamentalists. Thinking and feeling as a mature human being is difficult, frightening and sometimes quite lonely. It doesn't bear the same addictive, charged appeal that fundamentalisms offer: joining, belonging, certainty and *collective power.*. Thinking and feeling as a mature human is slower, more uncertain, sometimes faltering, but finally with a strength that comes from developing and moving and changing with seasons, a strength similar to that of an old oak tree.

Teresa had found her way, and had not had to drop her spirituality in the process. She still believes deeply in God and Jesus and in the importance and divine inspiration of the Bible. What she has "divorced" is the naive acceptance of the arbitrary interpretation of Bible or Christian doctrine that is based on limiting and controlling people as a political tool.

After her conversation with James, she found herself angry at herself for even briefly being 'suckered in' by his attempts to diminish and steal her judgment; then she felt anger at him. Finally she felt a kind of sadness that James, and other intelligent, well-meaning people like him, have to resort to trickery, to shim-shamming and the "name of the Lord" to hide from honesty with self and with other people. She saw his strictures in his thought and action as wastes of a human mind dormant under the weight of fear and repression. She was angry at him for his cowardice, but understood very directly the kind of fear of change and maturity that led him to "sever his mind" from the truth of human and divine diversity and tolerance. Had she not herself knuckled under the weight of "Church" for several decades?

She took a walk by the creek. Her sense of freedom and direct experience were uncanny. It seemed that the encounter with James and the remembrance of being jailed by Pathological Christianity had briefly poisoned her system, only for her to be born again to a life lived directly and immediately and deeply and intelligently. All of her senses felt awakened, and she smelled, even tasted the fragrance of lupine and sugar pine by the creek. She laughed aloud at the thought, "Thank God I am not a Christian anymore--that kind!", and remembered her friend Jane who had made a wry comment the other evening, "Thank God I have no religious training!"

It's a free country, and because it is, we need always to separate church and state to safeguard freedoms. One way that this can be done is to monitor services that are being offered to the public which are under the jurisdiction of state licensure for encroachments of religious indoctrination. Mental health services, whether by psychologists, counselors, marriage and family therapists or others, are services under the jurisdiction of the state for precisely this reason. We don't want cult activity being passed off as promoting the health and well-being of the individual or the society. Pathological Christian Counseling is cult indoctrination. It inevitably, despotically and purposefully robs the client of autonomy, self-reliance, intelligence and competence. *Any counseling or therapy which proceeds from a conscious blueprint for right thinking, feeling or behavior on the part of the client is psychological rape.*

When the therapist has ulterior motives for the client, or a design or vested interest in a client's thought, feeling or behavior, we use the term "conflict of interest." This means that the therapist stands to gain in some way rather than in professional satisfaction arising from competence if the client acts or believes a certain way. It also means that the client is blocked from being autonomous and self-reliant by some special interest or gain that the therapist can garner by the client's being his puppet.

Here is a simple and sadly common example of the kind of conflict of interest that can occur when the therapist identifies and acts on his personal persuasion as "Christian".

John comes in for counseling with Luke, who identifies himself as a Christian Counselor. His legal title is Licensed Social Worker and he is highly qualified by the work and preparation he has done and the licensure process to provide counseling and psychotherapy to John. Luke and John happen to go to the same church, but they don't really know each other. There is no conflict of interest here (as there would be, for example, if they were related or friends or had business interests in common).

John is 27 and has had dates with women, and once was engaged to be married, but has had for the last two years dreams, fantasies and feelings of attraction to other men; he has not acted on these as of yet. He is hoping through counseling to reach some peace about his homosexual longings, and believes in his own views that there is no irreconcilable conflict between homosexuality and Christianity. No one in the church knows about these thoughts or feelings--he appears to everyone to be a fine, eligible Christian bachelor "ripe for the picking" by some equally eligible young woman. He is an engineer and has a good position with an adventuresome electronic engineering firm in town.

John chose Luke to counsel with for several reasons. First, he has heard from other people in the church that Luke is a compassionate, understanding man, who also combines good professional competence and training. Second, Luke is a "committed Christian," and John wants to keep in the faith. Luke looks like one with whom he can speak in his conflicts, someone who would understand, since they share beliefs in common. Third, Luke reminds John a little of his father. Luke is about the same age his father would have been, but John's father died a couple of years back of a coronary, and in some way, John imagines that this will be an opportunity to feel closer and resolved with his father.

John finds that in the first three sessions, he cannot summon the courage to bring up his "real topic," that is, the conflict of his homosexuality and "being a Christian," but rather speaks about some depression and anxiety in general terms. He is testing Luke, (though he doesn't think of it in this way), against the more difficult moment, and trying to find if he can trust Luke.

Luke suggests some Bible passages to comfort John, and gives him some breathing exercises to do as well as some messages to tell himself about God's love for him. He suggests prayer time in the early morning before the day begins, and gives John a book of meditations on scripture to use for these morning exercises.

On the third session, John has nearly worked up his fortitude to bring up the "main topic," but is hesitating and stalling when Luke happens to mention something about a news broadcast that he had heard which was about gays seeking full recognition and acceptance in the military. Luke, perhaps out of an unconscious recognition that this was an important theme, goes on a short rave with not a little sarcasm about gays and states that God loves them anyway, but that they must see beyond their malady, join God and give up their homosexuality. Luke chuckles and says, "At least you and I won't have to worry about that problem, will we?" As he has done so many times before in other circumstances, John simply grins and shakes his head, acquiescing to the pressure to conform to the expected response. He manages to maneuver the topic to something he can discuss without fear, and narrowly escapes the session.

Alone at his house that evening, John finds himself in a terrible dilemma. He disagrees with his therapist and is afraid of his judgment. This in itself might be an opportunity for some very good personal development, and often is in psychotherapy. It might allow him to experience disagreement, the development of autonomy and personal confidence, if this were *good psychotherapy, but it is not.* Working out differences of opinion, conflicting feelings and emotional intensity may have been exactly the work that would give John the boost to work through his bind to his own judgment, and even to feel the kind of authority a son can work out over the years sparring with his own father, since Luke was a "stand-in" for John's own deceased dad.

But the "counseling" with Luke will never afford him these opportunities, since John cannot "risk" the encounter. Too much is at stake because of Luke's conflict of interest. John is not only afraid of Luke's judgment (normal in psychotherapy), but now afraid of damnation for "being a bad Christian", fearful of Luke spreading ill will in his church toward John, since John now knows he cannot trust Luke with his secret. Luke has a specific agenda for John, that is, heterosexuality, and will use any maneuver of colonization necessary to missionize him. John stands no chance of working out his own deep judgment in therapy with Luke because of Luke's stance. Luke can tolerate only "converts," not mature people, among his clients, so he can never serve as John's psychotherapist. Also, we see that Luke doesn't have the personal security to see John with tolerance, but *must* have him be a "Christian" in the mold that he sees proper.

A therapist must never have a 'meaning agenda' for a client, A psychotherapist must never have an agenda of "being right" with a client, since that is not his place. Perhaps it is the place of a parent of a very young child, or of a mathematics teacher or of an engineer of a bridge when he is instructing the foreman of a work crew how to properly distribute the stress so it won't fall down. Such a position, however, is never appropriate for a therapist, and it matters not at all what his own theory is. It sometimes happens that a therapist, *for the purposes of therapeutic drama and the development of the client's own sense of self* can "pretend" to know what is right or wrong for the client. He can "play act" a parent of a small child or the part of a god in the client's life, but he must be aware that despite his appearance of knowledge, consciousness or awareness, he *never, ever* knows in any absolute way what is right or wrong for the client. Therapy limps along in its own shy version of science, and science itself is a matter of one well-considered theory eventually being replaced by another, even better considered theory. Therapy attempts, with the best intentions and the best development of thinking and theory available, to help each person. The therapist hypothesizes or makes "educated guesses" about each person's life, and experiments or acts with each of these guesses to find out what actually works to help the person find deep satisfaction and productivity.

The dishonesty of all religions is that they attempt to solve the problems of each individual person with the most universal and general of tools, disregarding the wild, intriguing spectacle of the individual psyche. Attempting to solve all personal problems with passages from the Bible, the Tarot deck, the I Ching or even with a particular psychological theory is precisely like trying to do all mechanical work with a hammer. Something will get done, all right, but will it be what you hope for? It may be argued that there are at least two tools in

Pathological Christianity, i.e., prayer and Bible study, but there are two sides to the common hammer also, the blunt end and the claw, one for thumping things down, the other for pulling them out.

What are the tools of the honest therapist? They are the same as those used by the honest scientist. The honest therapist

- does not know the answers for you. Cannot tell you what will make your relationship good or your kids behave or your life fulfilled.
- like the honest scientist, is at his best when he is a good observer rather than a speculator; tells you what he sees rather that reading the future.
- never attempts to induct or indoctrinate you into his or her belief system, way of life, personal philosophy, entrepreneurship or Pyramid Scheme.
- tries to erode your certainty about life, to challenge you to be more thoughtful about yourself and others; neither mollycoddles your current views nor spoonfeeds you other ones. The minute a new certainty has developed, he goes to work to erode that one as well, until you express autonomy and strength on your own.
- recognizes that any advice or suggestions he or she gives you may well come from his or her own longing or fantasy life, and may have nothing to do with you.
- never brings his or her religious or political beliefs into the therapy room as a basis for any part of the therapy.
- recognizes that today's view of theory will be tomorrow's interesting, curious superstition.
- is intelligent and as well-read as she can be in world literature, religions, philosophies, natural sciences, political science or other knowledge which will help her establish a balanced position between *respect* toward the variety of

beliefs and feelings that humans can have and *an attitude of playful irreverence toward each and every one of them.*

"Christian Counseling" is not honest therapy

- "Christian Counseling" is really nothing more than political indoctrination, missionizing the natives, colonizing. It is a format for increasing the army of "Christian Soldiers," and not an approach to encourage, guide or deepen the individual's maturity in thought, feeling and action.
- The goal of "Christian Counseling" is social control, the control of individuals based on rules, indoctrination and fear, rather than on their developing integrity and maturity through increasing consciousness. It is based on the mistaken belief that human beings are incompetent on their own.
- "Christian Counseling" holds a profound disregard and distrust of private individual psychology and individual initiative, which (along with awareness of family and societal influence) are cornerstones of psychotherapy.
- "Christian Counseling" is unethical as a form of psychotherapy, since it "leads" rather than "follows" the client, and assumes that the client can never know (despite his or her age, maturity, life experience, depth of understanding, education or whatever) what is best for him or her. Only "The Bible," "Jesus" and the evangelist/"counselor" can know what is truly best for this miserable wretch.
- Pathological Christian Counselors have learned to look *assimilated*: have shed the image of "difference." You must be on your toes as a consumer of counseling or

psychotherapy services, because they have an agenda for you. Be sure to ask if a counselor is "a Christian" and then decide if you are ready to be second-guessed in every aspect of your life, looked on as a crippled heathen atheist if you don't follow their "biblical principles." These people have adopted the strategy of "normalcy" and infiltrated every profession. Remember their view, *they (along with their pal Jesus) know what is best for you; you don't know what is best for you.* Is that what you want?

How did Pathological Christianity develop its pathological perspective?

- Once Christians were "different" (at the beginnings of Christianity), punished, martyred, victimized for being Christians.
- Because they believed they were "special " and "in" with God, they developed a psychology of entitlement, uniqueness and superiority. Part of that superiority came from the belief that they had earned it by suffering for God.
- But then they got power (through the military dominance of Rome).
- This did not mean giving up the fantasy that they "suffered for their faith," and therefore were special.
- They discovered how to use the artifice of combining entitlement, victimization and power to dominate. It's a neat stratagem whereby "Christians" get to be superior and special in every way there is, since they believe they are still martyred (even after approximately two thousand years of total domination over at least half the world), still entitled to absolutely everything that exists for their own personal use

and believe that they have a right to rule every living being
and take dominion over everything there is and that this right
is given by God.

- "Christian Counseling " is training in using entitlement: it is
  missionizing. All clients (parishioners) learn is how to feel
  bad and how to make others feel bad.

*It is unethical for "Counseling" to be religious training.
It is a conflict of interest.*

*Any counseling or therapy which proceeds from a
conscious blueprint for right thinking, feeling or behavior on
the part of the client is psychological rape.*

*Therapists must never have a direct agenda for their
clients. The purpose of psychotherapy is to support patients to
find their own answers, their own way of thinking, feeling and
behaving*

B. Binds and Paradoxes: The Impossible Commandments.

The following are unresolvable binds, contradictory
commandments given by Pathological Christianity. The aim of
these cockamamie commandments is to keep followers
confused, sexually repressed, orderly, guilty, afraid, and willing
to surrender self. By their very unresolvability they force the
"Christian" into recognizing his or her incompetence.
Unresolvable binds of this sort are the meat and potatoes (or the
tofu and spinach) of every religious movement, since they are
the kind of traps that are offered us by our own understanding of
the complexity of life. They are problems of consciousness.

Life is paradoxical, confusing and mysterious in many
ways. However, there is an enormous difference between

admitting that life is a mystery and attempting to solve that mystery honestly and simply proclaiming that one has the answer to such mysteries based on one's personal psychology.

Religious or "spiritual" leaders pretend that they have achieved some mastery over the commandments by "surrendering to Christ," or "giving my life over to the Lord," or other such statements. The "secret that is never discussed" is that no one can actually fulfill these commandments. Some leaders are savvy enough to know this, and do not attempt to do so except in word only, carrying on lives rich with power, sex and 'high livin'. Other leaders are as confused, repressed and tormented as their follower, but continue to attempt to fulfill the paradoxes, since they sincerely believe that they are "God's Will." These are the *losers*.

Pathological Christianity has forwarded an answer for each paradox, and actually, it is always the same answer: don't try to answer what seems to be contradictions. *Jesus* has already given the answer, and all you need to do is follow the given Pathological Translation: *Brethren,* conform, do as I tell you (exactly!) and you just might get some of the goodies I have. You must do precisely as I say, and if you don't do things right, you will know it, since you will not get the palpable rewards that the *good* get.

In the little drama that follows, I have tried to portray a discussion of some of the basic binds of Pathological Christianity and how those are handled. Each *bind* is stated as a court case. Two advocates then have a little exchange. *Paul* is the prosecuting attorney, standing up for the (Pathological Christian) Company in its Crusade against Upstarts, Mollifiers, Liberalizers, Pagans, Freethinkers, Old Hippies, Heathens, Individualists, Anarchists, Heretics and other Criminals of the State. *Joseph* is the defense guy, standing up for the Accused, those heretical chaps who dare to think, feel as mature, autonomous individuals. Joseph does not defend pure anarchists or those who merely "do their own thing," but tries to give a reasoned and reasonable response that might be supported by an autonomous person. He only takes cases where his client has given careful and earnest thought to his or her position, views and actions.

Case #1. Surrender   vs.   Control Yourself
(also Feel Deeply   vs.   Be Careful)
      The bind:

You don't have any power or will of your own, only what God gives. You must recognize this right away and surrender to God. Meanwhile, control yourself, be good, do right!

Paul: I don't see any problem with this. The answer is clear. Give up the old self and become new. God is the Captain of the ship regardless of what you do. You will be in control of yourself and even risen up as part of the grand, glorious control of everything at the feet of the Lord, as soon as you have given yourself to God. Women must give themselves to God, husband and the Word, as men to God, wife and the Word. Children must give surrender to their parents. Control is surrender. God will show you the way.

Joseph: You are making a web of political power by portraying it as spiritual highfalutin' goodness. You are trying to steal a person's ability to think for him or herself by trapping and immobilizing him or her. You remind me of the movie *Gaslight*. A husband devises a plot to drive his wife insane. He keeps turning down the lights in the house and when the wife remarks that it is getting dark, he tells her she's crazy; she finally believes she is crazy. You are trying to drive people crazy by telling them they are unfit to think and feel and act for themselves and at the same time telling them to control themselves. The human being is more capable and competent than that. Any god who supports your plan to make people believe they are incompetent should have his head examined!

Case #2. Love Your Enemy   vs.   Win
        The bind:
We are commanded to love our enemy.   One might suppose that loving our enemy means tolerating, understanding and being willing to compromise and leave him to make his own decisions about what is best.   But Pathological Christianity requires victory, defeat of the enemy, vanquishing the Enemies of Christ.

        Paul: No contradiction. We love all people, but we hate the devil. Because we love people, we wish to free them from Satan's influence and bring them to a true   happiness. Correcting people and bringing them to Christ is an act of ultimate love. I recognize that it is hard for non-believers to comprehend this, but those in the faith are guided to special understandings. Once you have glimpsed this light, you will begin to discern the truth.

        Joseph: There are many truths, and I respect the fact that many people have felt a mighty jolt of wisdom, guidance and love from Christ. In my own apparently dull light, I see love as relinquishing the need to conquer other people, and to accept what others say brings them a good and satisfying life. When you tell me that to love someone is to vanquish him or her, I think of a father of a friend of mine who, while he was raping her, told her, "I am doing this to you because I love you and to show you how cruel the world can be." You are not doing me a favor to steal my right to think and feel as a mature human being, to try to make me feel inferior or afraid or doubt of myself because I don't share your opinions. Faith and prayer can inform understanding, I agree, but should not be a substitute for thinking, questioning, wondering, puzzling and coming to some answers that might work for me. But that doesn't authorize me to franchise my opinion as the one and only cure-all elixir.

Case #3. Don't Care About Money   vs.   Wealth=Goodness
(also:God's Grace is Boundless vs. He gives more to Believers)
       The bind:
       You shouldn't be concerned about how much money you have, since God will provide. However, it is evident that God provides better for some than others, and they are the ones God has chosen to raise up by rewards. So look at how God has rewarded you and you'll know if you are on the right track. Care about money.
       Paul: Jesus spoke more about money than any other topic. You aren't to love money but God. However, God is the source of all, so those to whom he gives money, as for example Mr. X who has three huge houses in California and Colorado which God gave him for his very profound and moving work in his ministry. You must put the interests of other people, people you serve, above your own; then, if God wants you to have money, he will make certain you have it.
       Joseph: You have created even more of a bind, rather than answering it. Money and love are confused in your picture, and the source of this confusion is a God who has forgotten he had a universe to run and got tied up in doling out Divine Welfare. Money is about political righteousness, not divine righteousness, though goodness knows we have the two intermingled. Something we might do more of is to find out what money means to people and what relationship they have to it. Money is something to care about--is it our father, mother,

friend, boss?, or--as it appears in your picture--our *God in the form of His Love and Reward to us?* Capitalism is based on seeing money as the love of God.

Case #4. Don't Have Pride   vs.   Pride In Salvation
   The bind:
   Don't be proud, but be proud.
   Paul: This is another clear-cut case, with no contradiction at all. You must see the difference between having self-pride and the pride of having Jesus in your life and having the right answers to all. You can be proud, immensely proud, of being saved, but the only good pride is the pride in being loved by Jesus and knowing it.
   Joseph: You should be ashamed of yourself for using *Jesus* as the name of your private little *tea-party club.* It is the most natural thing in the world for a person to be proud of accomplishments, of talents, of insights. The only purpose of squelching such personal pride is to combat intelligence and creativity and fun, the bane and *horror* of Pathological Christianity. There is an old expression "pride cometh before a fall." The only reason there is a "fall" (or better said, a depression) is because Pathological Christianity teaches you to feel self-hatred and guilt whenever you feel *enjoyment.* The natural state of pride is *enjoyment, excitement in discovery and the feeling of satisfaction that comes through evolving and changing and awareness.* Pathological Christianity fears and therefore always tries to take away pleasure. Pleasure is something private and ecstatic, therefore something that *cannot be controlled politically or economically.* For that reason, pride should be cultivated universally, to diminish the harm of Pathological Christianity. I don't mean *arrogance;* arrogance is the belief that you are better than others. Let's leave that to the

evangelicals. For the sake of the robustly human being, let's use another word for pride: _enjoyment!_

Paul and Joseph go on debating for several hours, in much the same way. Meanwhile, we step out for coffee and a donut. We look at our itinerary for the debate and see that they still have to consider the following binds:

- Think The Right Way (&   vs.   Don't Think
  bring honor to Christ)
- Use The Bible to Guide   vs.   The Right Path Is Set
- God Is Your Friend   vs.   Wants You To Obey
- God Is Love   vs.   People Burn In Hell
- Live Morally   vs.   You Are A Tissue of Sin
- Follow Jesus's Example   vs.   Don't Be Like Jesus
- Anything Wrong Is Your Fault   vs.   God's Omnipotence
- You Are Responsible   vs.   You Are Powerless

We sit and drink our coffee in silence. After a while, we start talking things over. The answers to these binds given by Pathological Christianity are not congruent with a people who supposedly have free will. Family therapists call such traps "Double Binds." The effect of such binds is pathology (there is disagreement about whether the effect of double binds on people in families is to produce whether psychosis or neurosis, but agreement that they produce pathology). The classic example is "Come here and go away at the same time!" Biologically, emotionally, psychologically, the person who tries to fulfill both commandments at the same time, since he cannot do so, is frozen and traumatized. How much more so if the "commander" is "God," and the simultaneous fulfillment of both sides of the paradox is absolutely demanded for well-being or even existence.

C. "Right" and "Wrong", "Godly" and "Ungodly"

Yet the leaders--the evangelists--are somehow "exempted' from the turmoil of these binds, apparently as a result of their direct relationship and partnership with God. They are granted the power and privilege of blamelessness of being "holy." They are given a special calm and certainty.

However, a sober perspective on human beings with all their personal psychology, their own foibles and difficulties and developmental conflicts reveals the following realistic view: *There are no holy people, there are no spiritual people; there are only people.*

There is a fantasy that the "godly man" or one who is able to successfully *portray himself* as having resolved these paradoxes is "of God." This somehow confers psychological, theological or political wisdom on them; they are given *carte blanche* to run other people's lives--all, of course, *in the name of God.*

Perhaps some evangelicals see themselves as **better than Jesus**. They speak with pride of all the things they have done, in Jesus' name, for his sake. Sometimes I get the impression that they are acting for the sake of a debilitated child, a man who perhaps didn't have the chutzpah to do all these things for himself, to get all these believers amassed, to get a big moneyministry going, to get political action committees, to get their name on television.

Language Games In Pathological Christianity

The Big Game in Pathological Christianity (not unusual in human groupings in general), is to try to be "in the fold" and not "out."   The place that is "in" is called "saved" or "born again," or with unbelievable arrogance and short-sightedness, merely "Christian." There is no real word for the "other place," except in negative terms, such as "Jim is not a Christian." The old phrase "Jim is a heathen (pagan, etc.)" is not used much anymore, as if to express the attitude that other ways of believing don't even have enough existence to merit a name.

If you do get defined as "A Christian" by Pathological Christianity, you get to enjoy certain idealizations that you live by and represent to the rest of the world. In one "Christian" university, all staff and faculty are required as part of their employment to sign a statement including among many other things: "I accept Jesus Christ as my personal savior," "I believe that the Bible is the literal Word of God," "I will not drink alcohol or do other acts which might portray me in any negative way to the non-Christian world, so that I may bring honor to Christ."

The purpose of these "oaths" is to make a Christian environment, one of grace, redemption and protection.   In practical terms, it results in a place of isolation, bigotry, conformity and condemnation of all other ways of living.

Mirages

These are a few of the *mirages* that are thrown up by Pathological Christianity

- Christians are "safe" and "nice"; safer and nicer than other people.
- Christians can be trusted in other areas of life to perform better, more thoughtfully, more thoroughly, more conscientiously, more compassionately, and with more

"value on the dollar" (their work is a good economic value). Thus we have "Christian Muffler Shop," "Christian Real Estate Agent," "Christian Athlete."

- If you are *saved*, some magical controls over your thinking take place.   You will be freed from thinking of "perversions" or of other harmful thought. You will think pure and noble thoughts of other people.
- God "prepares" people for marriage, operating a kind of mystical, heavenly matchmaking service. He is currently preparing "the one" for Suzie, her "future husband," and "the one" for Thomas, his "future wife."

As a psychotherapist, I have consistently come upon this last fantasy, whether in direct or indirect form. Evangelicals have apparently made overt a daydream that is in the fabric of Pathological Christianity and has been for a very long time. Born-agains are taught that they must save themselves for some particular mate that "God is preparing" for them. Others have a less conscious but still strong assumption that "there is one particular person made just for me"; another form this takes in New Age thought is that there is a 'divine complement' waiting out there for me.

In a way, this is a charming concept. It suggests that I am special and that there is one distinctive and perfect person for me--and that our unity will be sacred and sanctified.

In another way, it is a horrible trap. The effect on many people's lives is that it paralyzes them from enjoying dating, since they must be continuously asking the question, "Is this the *one?*" This kind of self-awareness is deadening to enjoyment or satisfaction. If you are not "sure" that this person is "the one," then you can't really appreciate or value being with him or her. That is a pity, and extends the "search" much longer than if you are simply paying attention to what your heart, mind and observation might tell you. Pathological Christianity, however, teaches us not to think or feel or act critically anyway, so how would one know? We only look for idealizations, projections, fantasies that fit a mold, so how can we recognize if we are having a good experience anyway? A good question, and an answer might be to do some maturing through good psychotherapy. Good psychotherapy will always focus on your developing the strengths of having your own mind and knowing your thinking and feeling.

So one trap is thinking *this is not the one*. But it can be just as much of a trap to think *this is the one*. The problem here is that you will idealize the person and the relationship. You will believe that God has waved a magic wand over it, that it is sanctified and holy. You will try to freeze-dry it, make it solid, permanent, unchanging and forever beautiful, magnificent and good. Then when the other person begins acting just like what he or she is, that is, *just a human being*, your disappointment is inevitable, and can destroy your confidence or your confidence in the other person, *because you haven't done it perfect*.

Many people conclude at this time that they just got the wrong person, and that the idealized, perfect one is still waiting out there. They get ready to ride the idealization merry-go-round another time, with predictably the same results.

Idealization is only useful when done with a sense of *fun*. When you know that you are idealizing someone or a relationship, doing it consciously, with tongue a little in cheek, with a little sense of irreverence and playfulness, it is a delightful game, very exciting and provocative. It doesn't get that stodgy, sticky seriousness that is just bound to result in some kind of disappointment and failure.

Shakespeare's play *Much Ado About Nothing* has a nice contrast between the two types of relationship. The young, dashing idealist Claudio falls in love with beautiful, saintly Hero. Their marriage is canceled in a scene of violence and hatred under the unfounded *suspicion* that Hero is not a virgin; the love between the two is a *mirage, based on perfection and idealism.*

The other couple, Benedick and Beatrice, are a little older and wiser. They are also a lot more fun. Their love is based on strong characters; each of them is skeptical and stinging and more than a little sarcastic. Each has vowed against love or marriage, yet finally, because those around them saw they'd work well together tricked them, they do recognize the fun and excitement of being around each other. Even as they marry, they jibe each other, play with each other.

I'd much rather bet my life savings on rich-blooded Benedick and Beatrice than on the pretty, cardboard idealists Claudio and Hero.

"Godly" and "Ungodly"

Abracadabra! The trick is that right "words" can get you in. An example is "I accept Jesus Christ as my personal Lord and Savior." Presto, you are in, and Jesus *goes to work* in your soul, making you right. He wanted to all along and was just waiting to do this for you, just waiting for your invitation. Jesus is your real partner, your real buddy. He won't abandon you. Just say the word and he will show, and never leave you. *He's not like those other guys!*

This appears benevolent, merciful, generous, yet the opposite applies--a wrong behavior or word gets you "out" (though there is always room for you to get back "in" if you will say the right words: "Bible, Jesus, Will of God, Prayer & Cetera).

However, a "right behavior", no matter how beneficial to mankind, to family, to nature, cannot get you "in" without the right words.

Pathological Christianity teaches that there is safety in language, in certain formulas, in magical incantations.   It requires that people remain in the developmental stage sometimes termed "the magical years," of roughly three to six years old, when kids think (appropriately for their years) that the cause for things happening is something called Magic. Witness the success of the book *All I Ever Needed to Know I Learned in Kindergarten..*   You will know all you need to know if you have certain Bible verses at the ready and can plug them in where needed , such as when you experience any uncertainty, fear, doubt, wayward thinking or feeling, when encountering an "enemy of the Lord" or defending values or ideologies you happen to prefer. You just wave your magic wand.

I remember a minister at the church where my family went when I was a young adolescent. He would not "say the right words." He was always saying things like "Why do we believe this?", which was supposed to be answered by any number of formulas such as "Because the Bible tells me so." However, he would say things like, "We believe it because we are too lazy to think! Think for yourselves, people. Do you believe it because you are lazy or stupid? Have you examined the contradictions and outright unprovable assumptions the entire Bible is based on? Are you ready to believe if the whole story is shown once and for all as a storybook fantasy?" I remember for the first time being absolutely awake in church. I remember grinning and looking around and being very, very excited, and thinking, *well this will be fun; I just wonder what old Mrs. Winkleman is thinking.* Mrs. Winkelman was pale as a ghost.

Then at prayer time, the minister sang "Twinkle, twinkle, little star." As I remember, he was there for exactly four Sundays, just long enough to express-transfer in a cardboard minister of the kind I was so used to sleeping through. I'd love to thank that minister for the only profound moment I ever experience in my youth in a church, and wish I knew his name.

Pathological Christianity cannot tolerate this kind of authenticity and directness. The only food it can stand is bland, pale rhetoric.

A true spirituality, a true Christianity, welcomes this kind of provocation and interesting challenge. In a spirituality worthy of any claim to universality, you need not think, behave, speak or feel *any particular way at all* in order to be 'included.' Any 'spiritual' perspective which requires *anything at all*, any change in the person of any kind, is not spiritual, but indeed *political.*

Four Forms of Tyranny Over Individual Thought

What are the philosophical roots of Pathological Christianity or of Pathological Spirituality of any form? Whatever squelches understanding, experience or individual competence. Each of the following Forms of Tyranny can be a form of fundamentalism, especially if it is believed without humor, in deadly seriousness. Each is an assumption about the basic "stuff" the universe is made of. Each claims to know what is real, yet not one has more final claim to truth than any other. Each of these positions is merely a "matter of preference" as a way of explaining what the universe is at base. Yet the adoption of one or another of these viewpoints makes a huge difference in how you act or ought to act.

Materialism

- Materialism: Insists that *everything* can be reduced to measurable, observable quantities, thus rejects mystical, intuitive or *quirky, inexplicable experience*.
- Also referred to as the "scientific view", though science is really just as mystical as other explanatory approaches in that it also proceeds from certain "unprovable" assumptions about reality, and applies a "measuring stick" that in itself is quite arbitrary, called the "scientific method."
- Materialism steals from the individual:
    a sense of wonder
    imagination and fantasy
    discovery and mystery
    empathy for other people, animals, plants, rocks since it reduces all to *empty thingness*
- Materialism promotes:
    cynicism about "weird" or "inexplicable" events or ideas
    isolation; if you are just *stuff*, you can't really imagine or have friends
    depression, since the world is just *stuff without meaning*.

    This tyranny can be called the "secular" tyranny.

Spiritualism

- Spiritualism: Insists that in the final analysis, everything is truly *nothing and nowhere*, except in the "spiritual" sense. Our essence (and in some traditions, the essence of all things

or beings) is ultimately spiritual. Thus, spiritualism rejects
the "scientific" view as only a small fragment of reality, and
certainly not explanatory of the ultimate reality. Usually it is
linked up with some kind of "cosmic plan" of one sort or
another. Everything is a mental concept, an idea, a part of
God, or a being in God. Part of the cosmic plan is that
ultimately every thing, being and entity is an extension of
God and God's Will (of course, this may be pluralized as
gods and gods' wills in some traditions.)

- *Spiritualism* steals from the individual:
    physical enjoyment, sense of trust in the body
    uninhibited sexual pleasure
    reveling in nature, images, the chaos, randomness and yet
  organization of nature
    humor   about   existence;   makes   everything   too
  "important"
- *Spiritualism* promotes
    idealization of people, places, things
    living in fantasy
    a delusion of superiority over others who are not
    "spiritual" by a certain definition
    isolation from others
    truckloads of guilt, since no one can live up to the
    delusions of spiritualism

This can be called the "spiritual tyranny."

Christian Dualisms:

- Christian Dualisms: Most things are matter without spirit, but humans are matter with spirit. Enormous problems are cause by the *clash* of matter and spirit, namely, they don't mix well. How to solve the problem? Mortify matter, since it is lower, ultimately unimportant, and really only a proving ground in which we demonstrate that we will not be tempted away from our true being, which is as spirit. So this is really another spiritualism, but with a twist: matter is allowed, but only in so much as God has given it to us to be scourged and mortified or spanked into obedience one way or another to "God's Will."

(the following are briefly outlined here, but spoken of in detail throughout the book)

- *Christian Dualism* steals from the individual:
  spontaneity
  fun
  imagination
  interest in one's personal idiosyncrasy
- *Christian Dualism* promotes
  self-hatred of body, desire, one's individuality
  psychosis (dissociation from one's self-identity and body)
  neurosis (alienation from one's self-identity and body)

Psychological Realism

- Psychological Realism: This point of view is really *dangerous* to established societies, because it is *anarchical.* Psychological Realism maintains that the question of reality doesn't matter at all (or perhaps, doesn't "spirit" at all?) There is just "something going on". Call it whatever you like, spirit, matter, Og and Magog, but the Psychological

Realists have no real need to "name" it at all. Psychological Realism simply stands in amazement at the fact that something exists at all rather than nothing. Psychological Realism is really the least tyrannical of these views of reality, because it doesn't attempt to supersede any other point of view, but rather allows and enjoys creative explanations or stories about what is. For the Materialist, Spiritualist or Dualist, the Psychological Realist is really *maddening*, since he couldn't care less about an answer to the questions of "what is it all?" The Psychological Realist knows that there is not *an* answer to what is, but *many*, and none is any better than any of the rest, except where it makes a better story. What floats the boat of the Psychological Realist is *good stories*. However, even Psychological Realism can be a tyranny, if its exponent *requires or otherwise coerces* other people to see things the way he does, if he tries to take away the certainty of the materialist or spiritualist, for example, rather than seeing every position, including his own, as *laughable, essentially absurd.*

- *Psychological Realism* promotes:
    imagination
    logic
    creativity
    critical thinking and critical feeling
    respect and tolerance for all points of view
    responsibility for one's own thoughts, feelings and behavior
    a mind open to knowledge.

The Jekyll and Hyde Syndrome:
A Fundamentalist Fable of Christian Dualism

Robert Louis Stevenson wrote the book _The Strange Case of Dr. Jekyll and Mr. Hyde_ in 1886 as a kind of Victorian moral fable about the importance of keeping control over our "dark side.". Though perhaps few people have actually read the book, just about everyone knows that _Dr. Jekyll and Mr. Hyde_ refers to two sides of the same person. Dr. Jekyll is a highly respected, socially prominent physician who begins tasting his own experiments in chemistry. The effect is to produce, over time, an alternate personality--Hyde--who embodies all the dark, foul characteristics lurking under the highly reputable and proper outer personality of Dr. Jekyll. Eventually, Hyde "takes over" and becomes the entire personality, and the fable is complete, since the purpose is to demonstrate the fatal and morally damnable effect of falling under the temptations of dark tendencies, addictions, depravity and the like. The message is black and white. There is good and there is bad, and you must guard yourself against the bad: insert _Satan_ for _bad_, and you have the entire message of Pathological Christianity.

Fundamentalisms have a single minded view of human personality. In fact, it is their hallmark. They claim, "_We_ can define right and wrong, and only _we_ can do so properly." Correct behavior is then acting to _do the right thing_ and to beat back and refuse the tendency to _do the wrong thing._ From this we can see that they recognize the power of the _wrong thing_ or _Satan._ The other key thing is that the _wrong thing_ is universally found active and viewed and practiced by _the other_, that is, by people who are not in the fundamentalism. Other people who are not members of the cult are then deserving of scorn, derision, perhaps pity--but in any case an attitude of superiority over these "others" is perfectly acceptable, even expected.

This is a reflection of the assumptions of Pathological Christianity. Pathological Christianity is anti-science, anti-passion, anti-intellectuality--"against science" and "for faith." The reason is that good science proceeds by openness, by conjectures and refutations, while Pathological Christianity cannot abide this procedure, since it is too threatening.

Pathological Christianity is "against science" and "for faith," which means adherence to right thought, feeling and behavior by an arbitrary standard. Jekyll "meddles with science", and therefore suffers a fall into evil. He falls out of "respectability." Much of what is considered "respectable" by us today is a hangover from the wine of Victorian prejudices. *The Strange Case of Dr. Jekyll and Mr. Hyde* is a story about those prejudices. It is a fable that speaks to fundamentalist fears of psychological realism, fears of an attitude which accepts, tolerates and finds value in *all* reality. What do we collectively consider good and what evil, respectable and monstrous? I believe that the Jekyll and Hyde story is very instructive about what qualities we in the West have associated with good and evil in our accepted assumption of Christian Dualism. Let's look at the qualities of Jekyll and those of Hyde in this light.

Jekyll	*Hyde*
• "collective man"	• "individual man"
holds popular opinions, anybody's ideal for a good man; distinguished but very conventional	is different from anyone else in appearance, strange, unique, recognizable in oddness, in action, in speech

- large

he is a big man; culture biased toward large men as shown by research in hiring and promotion practices

- light-colored

light complected, ruddy-cheeked, with a shining countenance: the "picture of health" according to the Anglo-Saxon vision

- older

more supposed "maturity", modeled on the image of "older and more respectable."

- small

Hyde is short and stubby; when he wears "Jekyll's" clothes, he cannot "fill in" the size: he's too "small" of a man.

- dark-colored

swarthy, dark, shadowy: Hyde goes against the culture's emphasis on "fair" complexion

- younger

is actually of indefinable age, but young, and because of this, he is additionally suspect of being irresponsible and reckless.

- well-formed

having the kind of dimensions, structure and countenance that fit the common ideal of a "good man"; well-formed means somehow virtuous or good. Research shows that we assign less blame, trust more, give more and believe more someone who fits the physical ideals of the culture. We suspect little bad in them.

- well-connected

someone who is well-known, who is "one of us"--also, someone who is extroverted viewed with high regard. We say, "he is very outgoing and friendly."

- "deformity"

culture automatically assumes that some kind of deformity (such as the hump on Hyde's back) is a direct signal of their maliciousness, dark intent, suspiciousness. Research shows that we assign more blame, trust less, give less and believe less someone who has a physical deformity. We are always suspicious of them as if the deformity were an outward signal of inward evil.

- solitary

Western culture in general, and especially American culture, does not trust introverts, regards them as suspicious, paranoid, and up to no good, apparently "hiding" in their own little world.

- "legal"

Jekyll is a "man with credentials", recognized by "the state" as having joined up with the state, and therefore a "useful citizen" (at least he has not "been caught" doing something wrong)

- "day-world"

someone who is out in the light is viewed as someone good, willing to "be in the light of day." J has always lived a well-ordered, polished bourgeois life, creating the image of a "good person."

- overt

as in the case of day and night, what J does is purportedly open, "above board". Of course he has a secret life (Hyde). Until this is found out, all assume he is "upright" and "correct."

- "illegal"

Hyde is a "man with no credentials," not recognized as having an identity by the state, someone not "within the law." Hyde does commit crimes, but he is after all only the dark side of Jekyll.

- "night-world"

Hyde operates at night, and the association with night or darkness is that it is the "unknown," therefore evil. Just because a thing or animal or human is out at night doesn't mean that there is something evil connected with it, but it is a prejudice we have.

- hidden

what is hidden we cannot readily identify or explain, so it is a terror to us; the culture rejects anything which cannot be directly explained; an example is the attitude of the AMA toward tribal medicines of the Amazon., or even toward psychotherapy.

- loved

Jekyll is loved, which is a word in this context meaning merely "familiar."

- hated

Hyde is hated in part because he is something different from what anybody conceives, therefore a "monster"

- born of society, culture

Jekyll is a product of expectations, the proper, no surprises, established and homeostatic; expected not to challenge the foundation; faith in the established, regardless of the fact that what is established was once revolutionary.

- born of experimentation

Hyde represents change, chance, a shifting foundation, "what happens when we tinker" or try something new. He is the ultimate "lesson" of the bad that can some of "experimentation"--again the horror of change or difference.

Pathological Christianity is pathological in part because it tries to make Jekylls without recognizing that Hyde cannot be "beaten back," defeated, destroyed or eliminated, even by prayer. We cannot be "saved" from the Hyde in our character, or by trying to portray ourselves somehow as above or beyond the Hyde in us. Hyde is not bad, nor is Jekyll good. Each is an image of the sides of our character; and character is merely character. No person can claim goodness or salvation or superiority--that is grandiosity or *delusions of grandeur*, the old word for psychosis. But neither can anyone claim some personal hold on badness or loss or inferiority. No one can claim "I am awful" or " I am a despicable person". Such thinking is also a *delusion of grandeur*, or a form of grandiosity.

People are only people, and Jekylls and Hydes, as well as
many other representations
of character, including those of Jesus, Mary, Joseph,
Solomon, and Abraham exist in each and every single person.
The integration of character which we call maturity means
developing the capacity to recognize the value and function of
Jekyll and Hyde in each individual, and not to try to "get rid"
of any part of our character.

When we try to make ourselves "pure," "good," "saved,"
we do the opposite.   When we try to eradicate flexibility,
difference, oddness, "badness," "strangeness" or the like, we
merely drive it into unconsciousness, where it has far more
power to influence us *continuously, deeply, permanently.* The
literature of the early saints of Christianity is full of the ravings
of monks and nuns who tried to scourge and purify themselves
"for Christ" and got nothing but dark dreams, visions, ill health,
pain, suffering, loneliness, torment, anguish and psychosis for
their pains.

In a discussion with various publishers of "Christian
children's literature," I found out that they were looking to
publish (at the demand of their readers and also on the basis of
their own views) stories in which "children don't have problems."
What minor problems they do have get solved by mom and dad,
and by speaking to Jesus.   These publishers didn't want stories
which involved divorce, violence, calamity or great suffering,
which they see as "having a bad influence" on children.   They
want to portray to the children a good, pretty, ordered world in
which problems can be solved completely and directly by
pastors, policemen, parents and teachers.   Their belief was

something like "if you portray it and they believe it, they will make it so."

This is pure and simple cruelty and abuse of children. It is an attempt to "fake them out" by playing Wizard of Oz, to create a cardboard world which ill prepares them for any sort of real life, and creates an absolute isolation and lie. Men in their middle years in America well remember the lies we were all told about the Vietnam War about the immense Vietnamese casualties and the way we were winning over them with few losses; and then the shock of realization that the whole thing was a tissue of prevarication to keep our "honor" shiny, while young men died, were mutilated, maimed and emotionally crippled in Vietnam. Apparently we don't learn, though, because people in this same age group are now supporting the principle of lying to children to "make them feel better about the world." Astonishing.

Even many schools of psychotherapy is influenced by this Wizard of Oz mentality. Many psychotherapists are being trained daily in methods of substituting tricks such as hypnotherapy or "trance-states" for the careful and thoughtful work of integrating awareness, working to bring unconscious material into consciousness, confronting misinformation, correcting distorted thinking (correcting Pathological Christian thinking, such as the fantasy that we can be Jekyll without Hyde). There are psychotherapists, good, intelligent people who should know better, that believe that little hysterical cures such as hypnosis, cathartic screaming, pharmacological tricks (psychiatric drugs) on the brain and the like can effect profound cures for ills in the individual, family and society. Tricks will never substitute for the careful, thorough self examination of prejudices, illusions, fantasies, dreams and projections that each of us tries to use to avoid mature responsibility for our own thoughts, feelings and actions.

> *You cannot be "rid" of Jekyll*
> *You cannot be "rid" of Hyde*
> *Only honest self-knowledge*
> *Can harmonize each side.*

E. Abuse of Psychological Data
The "Power of Prayer" Fallacy

Various religious "research organizations" have been providing "Christians" with results of "studies" which are said to prove that in addition to the profound and unquestionable metaphysical benefit belief in Jesus has in the afterlife and after the end of the world, it's also "good for you" to be a Christian. Somehow it seems important to get Jesus in the rankings as at least as important as Vitamin C, aerobic exercise, roughage and low fat diet in one's daily well-being.

"Having a belief system" is said to reduce stress and promote overall better health, by making one feel less anxious, depressed and put upon by the duress of living. This is the new pseudo-science argument for being a Christian, also used by "spiritualists" and others of many stripes. It is an appeal to the "practical side," which says " see, it is not only moral and correct to believe, it is also *good for you.*" This could be true in a the sense that being "settled down" by having a sense of certainty reduces anxiety or the feeling of alienation associated with depression. Studies focus on the direct effects of "believing" something, which settles down the nervous system, thus in theory putting less strain on the body and giving the old machine some more miles. Curiously (and this is something that the religious groups don't talk about much), the *content* of the belief doesn't seem to matter at all. If I believe that a pine cone contains special powers and is my guardian angel, protecting me against all harm, my nervous system and muscles will relax. *I will feel better.*

But what happens when the "certainty" crumbles? Saying I believe in, for example, the efficacy of prayer-- without flagging--may be quite possible for an extended period of time. But what happens when something overwhelms my certainty with a certainty of its own? I will experience both the anxiety of uncertainty and of self-blame if all my friends are well and I am ill, if those around me get increasing wealth and happy relationships and I remain poor and alone. Of course, evangelists have all the answers: merely pray more, bow to the will of Jesus, etc. All these answers are meant for social control of the individual who gets out of line; all waverers must get reprogrammed. They are not convincing, since they are just forms of the argument, "You should like green beans. If you eat enough, you will. Eat some more and start liking them."

The radiant health that comes from moral superiority and self-righteousness depends on the ability to maintain flexed and tense muscles of certainty without wavering. It is a form of machismo, and like machismo or any other form of denial, is a terrific source of heart disease, cancer and other psycho genetic illness.

What of those who cannot afford certainty? Certainty is very expensive and requires much buffering from the world. Only the wealthiest evangelist can afford certainty or the kind of "health" it provides. This "health" is at the cost of the money, efforts and individuality of the congregation, as well as the natural resources and governmental control. This "health" requires armor, a castle and a moat.

It does not appear to me that Jesus was trying to provide a "security system," but rather a system of self-confrontation, presence to danger and death, a kind of fundamental undercutting of everything sane, careful and clean. He was not playing the Philistine game, but ultimately challenging all "traditional values." He was breaking up the game. He said *I come not in peace but bearing a sword.*

Pathological Conditioning

Much of modern psychology was developed during World War I and World War II, for the purpose of training people to be unfeeling about human craziness, violence and absurdity in war and to help people accommodate to it. Especially in World War II, psychologists wanted to evaluate very quickly if men were "fit for battle," which meant that they were not overly bothered by the notion of getting mutilated, dying or seeing friends tortured and killed as a result of making the world safe for Christianity.

A formidable literature grew up out of the researches of both Allied and Axis psychology, and one of the major discoveries was that people can be systematically and specifically conditioned to think, feel and behave in quite predictable ways, at least temporarily. Much psychological technology blossomed from these findings during the war and after, among which are concentration camps (and their equivalents), systematic propaganda, businesslike methods of physical and emotional torture, terrorism, psychological evaluation tools, use of radio (later, TV) news as a method for controlling political imagery, centralized and routinized public education, and *advertising*. The goal of all these procedures is to eliminate the creative, autonomous individual and regularize the citizen to a set of norms, determined by some source as being higher and greater than any individual might have on his own. The assumption is that the individual tends toward evil and misdeed, so the collective (Church, the State, the Company) must take charge and rein him in.

Conditioning has always existed, but its processes and methodologies have never been used in such a highly conscious and deliberate method to produce specific pre-determined outcomes. The Inquisition is the closest mirror to modern conditioning we have; and for all its gruesome fascination to modern viewers, its methods were simple hackwork compared to the exquisite psychological and physical techniques employed today to keep people in line. Furthermore, the total numbers of people affected by the Inquisition are minuscule compared to the victims of modern conditioning. Perhaps most importantly, the Inquisition did not subject every single citizen every single day of their lives to its shrewd and purposeful manipulations through every angle of television, radio, print and mail barrage possible as do the various users of modern conditioning today.

In its more benign forms, conditioning has been used to good effect to help "cure"(whether it cures or displaces the problem is controversial) patients of self-destructive behaviors, phobias, obsessions and compulsions. When used in psychotherapy, the ethical use of conditioning is where it "follows the lead" of the patient, that is, when it is used to help the patient in finding the relief he or she is seeking. The truth is that we do not know the net effects of conditioning on people's lives in general, and that working on an identified symptom or on conditioning a behavior may well cause him or her greater harm by displacing the symptom to an even more dangerous place. A simple example is that many times when people stop smoking through a program that does not emphasize awareness of thoughts and feelings as well, they begin overeating and may threaten a state of health that was already vulnerable through smoking by a new assault on the body.

However, more germane to our topic of Pathological Christian Conditioning are the more malign versions of conditioning, which involve determining an outcome without the permission of nor discussion with the recipient, and then simply going to work on him to get the results that are *for his own good and which are profitable to the Company.*

It is easy for Americans to see examples of despotism or violations of human rights in other countries. We trot about the world with our huge weapons setting other countries straight all the time. It is one of our favorite activities, along with pouring concrete, spending money, suing each other, and watching mindless movies, since all these things give us a distraction from personal self-analysis and help us avoid the pain of individual creativity and autonomy.

More difficult is to see the tyranny over individuals inflicted by advertising, our own government, our school system, and in particular, our Pathological Christian assumptions and evangelism. It is like observing our own eyes, which cannot be done without a mirror; yet we look at other religious and political perspectives, which are us in the mirror, and call what we see *those other people, the barbarians, the foreigners.* This is not a peculiarly American trait, of course. It is inherent in all systems of religion and government and all commerce. In commerce, one might say that it is justified that profit and control is king, since that is the purpose of business, but responsible thinking holds that business is not an activity separate from other human endeavors, and businessmen ought to think of themselves as servants of the race and the planet equally as much as teachers or ministers.

Paradoxically, the evangelical side of Christianity is about tyranny and conditioning, not about tolerance or love. Missionizing in any form, if you consider it well, is inevitably about dominance, superiority and self-righteousness.

Evangelicals do their work "in the missionary position," that is, "on top." However, like the winking Jesus, they often portray themselves as "on the bottom," the lowliest of men, once the most sinful but now saved by the blood, and therefore *armed and dangerous in the army of Jesus.* This is how the pump is primed, the first step in inculcating the unwary. For today's evangelical Christian leaders are students of human psychometry. They know their demographics and their organizational psychology. The first and foremost principle in conditioning is to know that a leader who is one of us will be most readily accepted and followed.

So the mechanics of conditioning that follow from this principle are simple. We know that people have a universal desire for permanent happiness, for wealth and security, for power and for belonging. What a leader must do is demonstrate to people that they are not *really* happy, secure and powerful, a job which is inordinately simple. Once the desire has set in for these things, in other words, when we are born out of the womb into the chilly and threatening world, we are ready for any way possible to return to the womb, as long as we remain babies. Most people remain babies all their lives, since thinking, feeling and behaving on your own are tough undertakings.

The birth of Professional Religion occurs when the first person recognizes that regardless of the fact that he cannot really provide for these needs for himself, he can convince someone else that he can. His follower gladly gives money, time, attention and pins hope on the leader, who thus gets the things he wishes--wealth, security and power-- at the cost of the follower. The follower is further impressed by his leader's radiant look of self-confidence, and continues to fork over his money and personality, hoping to be like the leader. The secret is, he can never be like his leader, since his leader exists by feeding on his flock and not by any real autonomy or strength of his own.

The leader--let's say minister here to make it quite clear-- clears himself of pride and suspicion of thievery of his congregation by giving the glory to Jesus, whose confidential phone number only the minister himself knows.

It is no sin that each person desires wealth, belonging and happiness since life is often cruel and stingy, breaking our hearts in a flash. But this is no excuse for Pathological Christianity, which supplants the hardships of nature with the promise of relief and certainty which are conditional upon the surrender of its followers' hearts, minds, souls and dollars, and are at the end of an endless maze of impossible binds and paradoxes.

Here is the essence:
- You want to be wealthy, happy, powerful and right.
- There is a way to achieve this. You simply pray and follow God's will. If you do things *right*, God will "raise you up according to his Will.".
- If you get what you are praying about (wealth, happiness, power), you are in accord with God's will. If you don't, then you are on the wrong track.
- If you are unhappy, powerless or poor, it is your fault, since God wants to raise his people up. *You have screwed up, and you will have to start over again.*

Pathological Christianity is a Pyramid Scheme with all the flock seeking the reward which will never come, paying in all the energy, attention, money and devotion, while the leaders get all the goodies and justify their booty as deserved since they are "godly." Have you ever wondered why so many pyramid schemes, lotteries and gambling are successful enterprises, even when people are totally apprised of the odds? It is because of Christian conditioning. The psychological principle is this: sacrifice now and you will get a reward later, the check will be in the mail tomorrow.

Pathological Christianity has discovered the methods of The Company Store. This is the process whereby an apparently magnanimous patron gives a job to an unsuspecting chap way out in the boonies where there are no grocery stores or prostitutes and then sells him what he wants at more than he earns, so that he is forever in debt, and the more he works, the deeper he digs himself, until he is imprisoned. A glance at the family credit card account will tell many people all they ever need to know about this gambit.

Well, there is an even better way of practicing The Company Store than that discovered by Master Charge or Visa, and it is employed by Pathological Christianity. With a credit card, you actually get some product for which you become indebted, say, a new television set. With Pathological Christianity, you get only promises of wealth, power and happiness, and nothing at all but a load of self-blame, disappointment and rhetoric, and membership in a club full of other people full of self-blame, disappointment and rhetoric.

Self-blame is inevitable in Pathological Christianity. How can one play the part of "godly person" all the time? Pathological Christianity demands an unflagging attitude of gratefulness to God, steady temper, refusal of anger, a constant beating back of the dark and the natural, as personified in Mr. Hyde. You must always be on the lookout for the influence of Satan and Secularism., This means not only outright violations of one of the Ten Commandments, but also anything which is not couched in evangelical language or which smacks of individual thought, feeling or behavior. Such individual initiative, or even the thought of such initiative is grounds for self-blame, which in itself is not allowed, since one must substitute prayer instead.

When we substitute a programme for being humans, eventually the full range of our humanity begins bleeding through anyway, despite our best efforts at suppression. The most frequent result of permanent grinning and "amens" and "thank the Lord's" (along with constant attention to one's thoughts and feelings to make sure she is "godly") is anger which flows downhill, carving its way through people with less power than the "godly one." In many cases I have seen as a psychotherapist, the recipients of the anger of evangelists are often their wives and children.

Linda showed up at my office one bright Tuesday morning, having told me on the phone the day before that she wanted to talk about "depression" she'd been in recently. After a few minutes, it became clear that she wanted to talk about her husband, Harold (known at the church as Doctor Wainwright), the rector of a local church. She was worried about him and about their marriage; she also had gotten quite terrified by some feelings and images that had "come over her" recently, namely, she found herself wishing Harold would "get in an accident and die." Last week, when he came home quite late from a Finance Committee meeting, she had found herself really excited at the possibility that he had been killed in an auto accident. She even had found herself sharpening kitchen knives with the images in her head of stabbing good Harold while he slept in front of the television set some evening.

Now Linda was horrified at herself. She was a woman who had always been immaculately proper, graceful and generous at all times, showing nothing but good will toward everyone around. She taught kids at Sunday school, volunteered for the board of a nonprofit agency for the disabled, and had even written a book entitled *Women of Grace*, which was a collection of portraits of famous Protestant women and their accomplishments. She got awards from two city agencies for her contributions to homeless shelters and for a program she did on the radio encouraging better race relations.

Linda's conditioning as a woman of her culture and as a "Christian" had certainly taken seed and grown quite a garden. Her conditioning had taught her to exclude negative thoughts/feelings, especially anger and rage. In order to qualify as a "Good Christian Woman," she was working overtime to put the lid on any anger or frustration she had at her husband, to give it over to the Lord. Never mind that Harold had not actually touched her, sat with her and had a long talk, taken even a little weekend trip for a vacation (it was always work), let alone made love with her. In the early days, they had tried to have a family. Linda miscarried several times and then developed complications which prohibited childbearing. They had never spoken about this disappointment,. Linda had asked Harold for at least five years if the two of them might see a marital therapist together, even if, to protect their "image" they had to go to some other town to see someone. He'd refused every time, saying that he was "quite happy," and that he "loved her deeply, as Christ loves the Church." He had a standard little speech for her, in fact, a short version of one of his sermons, which he delivered in these moments, something like,

"You know, Linda, when the intense infatuations and fires of the early days of romance in marriage settle down into the comfortable slow glow of embers, even if you do not feel the same excitements, it is the way to know that your love has changed from "being in love" to a deep "loving", a state far deeper and more spiritual than the ephemeral infatuations. A couple can grow in Christ, and leave aside the worldly needs, the requirements of childish reminders, that they love each other. You know I love you, or at least your spiritual side knows it. Please try to put aside these more petty thoughts about seeing a counselor and deepen with me in our love of Christ."

Even with the patronizing and demeaning tone and attitude with which Harold dismissed Linda, she was shocked at herself and at the strength of her fury at him in these moments. Of course, a "little anger" was acceptable, but this much was only to be "given to God" for Him to apparently recycle into fine feelings of grace and gratefulness, the ultimate kit model of emotional ecology. Linda was caught. Harold was a "good man," a man of God; everyone said so. She could point to no overt abuses or evidence of mistreatment. Everything she was feeling *must be her own sinful, ungrateful selfishness.* Linda thought, *I must be crazy, I must get some help to get over being crazy.*

As a good "Christian" woman, Linda had been trained to "support her man" regardless of any attitude of his toward her feelings or her well-being. Even if he had struck her or committed other violent acts against her, her approach to him would still require an attitude of forgiveness and an attempt to bring him back to Jesus.

Despite her intelligence, industry, accomplishments and her obvious contribution to her church, to her community and her family, she was still beaten down by Pathological Christianity. Even though she was furious with him, Linda felt that she was not really "good enough" to "deserve" Harold, that somehow she would never measure up to what the wife of Harold should be.

Harold had his Doctorate, and people in the community called him Doctor Wainwright. He was quite handsome, fit, and had a strong singing and speaking voice, which he used to good effect in his sermons. He dressed in well-tailored suits, which looked good on him; though he was 55, he was in excellent physical condition. She had no idea where he got the money for the suits. She later found out that they were gifts from a woman parishioner who owned a clothing store.

Harold had pretty extensive training in pastoral counseling, and served as a counselor to many parishioners who had lost their way emotionally and spiritually. With only two or three exceptions, the people who came to see him were women. As a matter of fact, he often played golf or even went to the galleries with some of these women. He swore he never had sex with any of them, but as far as Linda was concerned, they were still "affairs" because Harold gave them the excitement, fun and attention that Linda herself longed for.

Linda had gone so far as to blame herself for Harold's apparent "disinterest". She believed that she should be able to do something to make herself attractive to him, to create desire in Harold, so that he would want to spend time with her. She thought of herself as *boring, stupid and homely*, and she was none of these. Her conditioning had taught her to find fault in herself, since the whole approach to responsibility of sin, guilt and blame led her to the conclusion that someone must take the fall. Since everyone but she thought that Harold was the ideal and perfect husband, it must be she, Linda, who was crazy.

Meanwhile, Harold referred to Linda in sermons in the church as "my perfect wife," and spoke of how "fortunate and blessed" he was that God had seen fit to bestow upon him, a miserable sinner and servant of the Lord, the gift of Linda as a wife. He used little illustrations from their daily life to show how much he had learned from her about "the grace of God." He praised her and said that he didn't deserve her. The irony of all this made Linda's head swim. The women in the church swooned, what a man, what a husband, and were forever telling Linda how lucky she was to have a man like Harold.

Pathological conditioning kept building prisons around her, making her feel crazier each day, more self-doubting, more self-critical. She was trapped, and anything she would try to do surely would help build a more complex and subtle and more powerful imprisonment for her.

Of course, she had prayed every day to God to make things better, to make her a better wife for Harold, to make her adequate and good enough for him, to show her some path or sign that would help her along to being what Harold wanted. It often happens that as a result of the conditioning of Pathological Christianity, women are strapped with the burden and responsibility to "make things better" in a marriage or in the family. Apparently this is "woman's work." Besides, when a man holds so much power, is esteemed so highly, is given privilege, respect and adoration, why should he want to rock the boat by going to therapy?

Most men have the view, conferred by Pathological Christianity, that if something is wrong in a marriage, it is because the woman is not being woman enough--that she is being a nag, that she is simply expressing the natural dissatisfaction of women. It simply never occurs to most men--or if it does, they suppress the thought quickly--that they might honestly and forthrightly attempt another way of relating to women in order to contribute to the development of a marriage. If they have the thought, they then exaggerate their own blame, and start pouting and whining about their "being a total worthless bum."

Blame, sarcasm and sneakiness in relationships are the direct result of Pathological Christianity; they are the direct result of idealization, salvation, illusions, conditioning.

It is quite common for women to come to therapy with two wishes in mind: to make themselves more appealing to the men in their lives, and to figure out something to do to make the men in their lives be more attentive to them. She says that his original spark of passion seems to have extinguished (though she still loves him--or wants to) and she is trying to make it flicker again. She feels something is wrong with her, since she can't get his attention. She knows something is wrong with him, because he is always complaining about work, about being tired, about all kinds of things, but rarely or never shows any tenderness or interest in her anymore. She is bored, angry and sad, but believes, like any well-trained woman, that it is her job to fix things up in the marriage. She gets herself off to a therapist in the hopes of finding some answers.

Meanwhile her husband not only lacks appreciation for her efforts at helping them out, but is upset at her for spending the money, though he may have recently bought a new truck, some tools and a new shotgun for far more money than a few counseling sessions might cost.

Linda eventually decided to leave Harold, at great personal cost to her. When she told him she was thinking of leaving, he said to her that she would "profoundly regret" her thought, and certainly would never get away with leaving him. He informed her that she would be seen as a slut and ingrate by the church, by her friends, by God and by himself as well. When she said she'd rather not leave but would prefer to work things out with him, Harold said he'd always pitied her and prayed for her, and that as far as he was concerned she could stay, since it was "God's Law," but that there would never be any talk of counseling or "working on the relationship" or any other nonsense of the type, since the answer was clearly that she had not been faithful in her spiritual development.

Linda looked at him in astonishment, as if looking at a complete stranger, a man utterly unknown to her though they had lived together for thirty four years. He had no sense at all of what she was saying, what she had sacrificed of herself, how she had ignored his life with other women, the ignominy and embarrassment she felt in church when he painted those pretty pictures of their "saintly marriage."

Even after a year away from him, very good experiences with male and female friends who love and appreciate her, a man who completely adores her and treats her like a fellow and equal human being, Linda still feels as if there is something deeply wrong with her that couldn't "make Harold" love her. Such is the strength of Pathological Christian Conditioning. As Harold predicted, the parishioners (with two exceptions) turned against Linda, telling her they'd "pray for her," then never calling or visiting her. One of the women Harold was "dating" while they were married, a golf partner, called Linda one day and told her that Harold was just incredible in bed and had been for years.

Linda was surprised when she was offered a good job in a local social service agency, one she didn't even apply for. The director told her that he'd always seen Harold as a phony and Linda as a person of great integrity, and a person with "real spirituality," not the kind merely used as a form of self-serving power over other people or as a way of getting money.

Pathological Conditioning and Money

The Japanese save a considerable amount of their income. Why? They don't have Christian conditioning, therefore know that the power, money and happiness that you acquire are gotten through personal influence, hard work and family ties, not through "miraculous interventions by God." But the Christian West is driven by *salvation*, by a fantasy that some day God will get things right for me.

This fantasy is continually fueled by evangelists, who often use the *autobiographical method of conversion*, that is, portraying their own lives as stories of salvation. The salvation itself, where they turned the corner to power, belonging and wealth was less related to some spiritual infusion by a divinity than by the cold recognition that they could live at their ease digesting the fat of the congregation.

Are all evangelicals or all ministers wealthy? No, only the ones with least conscience and the best theater skills. All evangelicals live on the good will of Christians followers, some in cushier digs than others. Surely there are evangelicals who modestly and humbly goes about their work, invading no one else's world, but living by the word of God? But who can resist the allure to make good money, be admired and superior to others? It takes a very psychologically mature person to do so. This mature person must not be driven by narcissism.

Christian Narcissism

What is *narcissism?* People commonly confuses the word with *selfishness* or *egotism.* While there is some similarity, there also are important differences. An egotist is someone who thinks the whole world revolves around him or her, and that he or she is the most important and praiseworthy person around.

A narcissist is also focused on him or herself, and on getting attention. It looks as if he clamors for this attention because of self-centeredness and vanity, but he is actually hiding an overwhelming sense of emptiness inside. What happens is that he swings wildly and exagerratedly from one side to the other of something called *grandiosity.* At one moment, he is acting and talking as if he is the best, brightest, most important contribution to humanity that has been born; the next moment (especially after criticism of any kind), he is acting and talking as if he is the worst of all humans who have lived on the planet. He never or rarely has an accurate sense of his own worth, but exaggerates in turn between one pole of extreme importance to the portrayal of himself as loathsome refuse.

Pathological Christianity encourages this wild oscillation, and the sense of emptiness that goes along with it. It does so by confusing people or binding them to two extreme measurements of worth. On the one hand, it says, you are innately evil and worthless, a tissue of sin and hopelessness without Christ. On the other hand, you deserve and can get for yourself (thanks only to Jesus, not because of any merit in yourself), the ultimate jackpot--eternal life, salvation, total, unconditional love and acceptance, unperishing comfort, meaning and supreme value-- simply by signing up and "giving your life to Christ." Being taught this exorbitant set of extremes about human life creates in a person a fundamental confusion which is narcissism, the inability to measure one's actual talents and contributions, and to have a constant and realistic sense of self.

A person who endorses these two definitions of a person as innately sinful and lost but entitled to the most extreme of rewards through an absurdly small effort will have a great deal of trouble finding a sense of self-worth or any value in responsibility for him or herself. He or she will feel worthless, yet entitled to everything there is. This is the formula for creating a society of crime, welfare, abuse of others and refusal to take responsibility. Many evangels blame the ills of our society on "godlessness" or lack of Christ, but it is fundamentally the narcissism resultant from Pathological Christianity itself which is at root in a society of irresponsibility, since the individual person does not and cannot see how fundamentally responsible he is for his own acts. A belief which teaches "giving over my life to the Lord" and that "I deserve all rewards because of some other person (Jesus) but that I am at base evil" creates by its very definition a society of irresponsible citizens.

Pathological Christianity creates a sense of superiority in people, but one that is based on the market share of the thing which makes one superior--a secret ingredient called Jesus. Once Jesus has saved me, I deserve everything. Pathological Christianity is thus the belief system that has created a fantasy of the welfare state, the belief that everyone owes me a living. All I need to do to qualify is to give up my own individual thinking, feeling and acting, to "let the Lord control my life," in order to qualify for deserving everything there is, including the service, money and adoration of all other people, despite my purported "worthlessness." Hell, *I'm saved.*

In practice, however, it turns out that only a few people really get the goodies. These rich souls clearly deserve what they have even more than the hoi-polloi, although each

Pathological Christian is waiting for his ship to come in, to win the lottery or get to heaven. As Ken Kesey said in the 1960's, "Everybody wants the Revolution, just as soon as they get the ultimate stereo system." The fundamental Christian belief in entitlement creates a lot of empty, guilty souls waiting around for "something to happen." It creates a society which loves television, spectator sports, fast automobiles, big boats and endless stimulation through drugs, alcohol and "entertainment." Pathological Christianity creates a society in which people use hypnotherapy and Prozac and other psychopharmacological or medicinal artifices rather than face their own self realistically and stop living in delusions, trance states or fantasies of the future.

Christianity teaches that God has a Plan for the Universe, and that this Plan is constantly unfolding unto an apocalypse and final transformation. In Pathological Christianity, the individual soul is an anathema to the Plan. God has also a Plan for my soul just as he has Plan for the universe, which will finally unfold into eternalness.

How utterly shocking it is to people for whom things do not go well after they have "been saved," who get terminal diseases or have people desert them or are hated or never get a job promotion or win any contests or get elected to anything. The question then becomes something like *why did this happen to me?*

The Pathological Christian answer is *God wills it this way.* If I see things this way, I still get to be "special." God has chosen me, is testing me, is showing me something important. Do you see that this is merely another form of narcissism, the refusal to see oneself as an ordinary creature, one animal in a great experiment in organic forms? Entitlement and its corollary narcissism run deep, and no one is willing to be ordinary. A long time ago in America, the grade "C" in school stopped meaning "average" in a just fine or good enough sense, and began to represent some kind of problem or negative. A concert can no longer have value if it is rated "all right;" it must be assessed as "great" in order to have any importance at all. An entitlement culture, a culture of narcissism, requires a vast amount of stimulation and hyperbole in order to avoid looking at its emptiness.   If we look at American art, music, architecture, literature for very long, and set it up along the aesthetic products of other cultures, we find it empty, shallow and without soul.

Pathological Christianity fosters the belief that since "I" am special (being a *Christian*) the normal pains of life should not apply to me; I should always be granted a reprieve. Even fugitives from crimes, once they are apprehended say, "I have suffered long enough by having been on the run, and not being able to listen to my stereo, so I shouldn't have to go to jail." A woman in California brutally murders a man who is standing trial while he is sitting in the courtroom, and then she wishes to claim that she is innocent because she was "temporarily insane" due to having allegedly suffered injustices in her childhood. A man jumps into a speeding truck on the freeway holding his child; the child dies; then the man wants sympathy for having felt so depressed. A drug addict is beaten by the police. The drug addict wants sympathy because he had a hard life in his neighborhood; the police want sympathy because the man was acting strange and they have a hard job. An extraordinarily fat woman who will not confront her food addiction and consumption of huge quantities of food wants to be accepted and seen exactly the same as everyone else and not judged any differently. A prostitute who also offers "phone sex" to teenage boys thinks her occupation should be seen the same as anybody else's self-employment business. A man in a wheel chair gets enraged because he has to wait one minute to use the wheelchair stall in a public restroom; a non-disabled man was using it; this, even though all the other men waiting to go to the toilet had to wait five minutes or more. A church votes to exile a woman from their congregation because she is divorcing her husband who is an alcoholic and won't get help; she's going because she wants to protect her children, but "divorce is wrong."

All people experience what is called "existential pain." There is a story that a Buddhist woman's son died. She asked the Buddha to restore her son to life. He said he would if she could find even one person who had not experienced profound grief. She tried for several years and found no one, and came back to the Buddha, thanking him for showing her ordinariness. This is not like Pathological Christianity, which teaches us to believe that God is making some thing happen for his believers which is different than for non-believers. Buddha did not suggest she should praise him or show him gratitude for her losing her son, but instructed her to find what she was going through as ordinary and normal; that deep grief and pain are not visited on any individual as some kind of "lesson," or part of some "Plan," but merely as part of what life includes, along with pleasures and discoveries.

Pathological Christians are taught to believe that they are special, so that even loss or suffering is somehow particularly glorified and makes them superior. This has been going on since the days of the Christian martyrs, who found their own masochistic way into death "for Christ," and gloried in their own sufferings as somehow "holy." The model, after all, is Jesus on the Cross, and many evangels like to see themselves on the cross today. They will even portray themselves as downtrodden, rejected or miserable to ennoble their "ministries." In fact, the more they are scorned, the better they like it.

There is a bumper sticker and T-shirt slogan referring to Christ on the Cross. It reads, "His Pain Is Your Gain." The image refers to the belief that since Jesus died on the cross, all who believe in him and in his work are redeemed and made supernatural and immortal like him. This is something like a "lose weight while you sleep" plan: it is another promoter of narcissism. Pathological Christians are lazy. They do not want to think or challenge or feel deeply. They want it all to be given to them. Because they feel entitled (our culture of narcissism) they love the simple "do nothing" view of Jesus having "done it all". They love the story of the prodigal son, who went out, partied and came home to his father, who still gave him half of his possessions, even though the elder son had stayed behind and worked hard all the time the kid was gone.. *Make no mistake, the welfare state is a product of Christianity. Christianity will never be able to heal the welfare state, since in its premises, it encourages and even extols entitlement.*

Pathological Christians wish to "identify with His pain." Why? Because they wish to identify with a grand, unending, total pain. Every person has existential pain, the basic pain of being born, of aloneness, of our having to find meaning for ourselves. Pathological Christians, because of entitlement, focus on and magnify their own existential pain and use this identification with a deity to make it appear special, unique, grander than that of other people, by connecting it up with Jesus. This gives them the right to identify and belong to some ultimate Plan, thus making their own experience profoundly significant. The Pathological Christian suffers--but from what used to be called "delusions of grandeur"

Nonetheless this doesn't help "heal" the direct experience of grief, despite the fact that it is advertised to do so. The effect of this sense of entitlement is dissatisfaction with everything of this world--a sense of isolation, being cut off from expressing natural emotion and the alienation of the individual from his own powers of thinking and feeling for himself. Superiority, or the fantasy of superiority, always has a price: the estrangement of a person from others. Knowing you and your beliefs are ordinary--no worse nor better than those of other people and cultures--promotes both self-acceptance and tolerance of difference in other people.

Now the belief that one is special, gifted and particularly important is not necessarily a bad thing except when it includes expecting others to serve this grandiosity, to feed it, to "adore" the Christian as one "adored the Christ child." Pathological Christians want to be adored, thought special, thought unique, thought worthy and *entitled* of whatever their whims happen to indicate

Perhaps even in the model of Jesus himself, at least in the events we know of his life, we can see the flaw that leads to entitlement. We know that he was "adored" at birth, considered totally unique, special and powerful. We know that he went into the temple at age twelve and completely overwhelmed his elders with his knowledge and understanding of Jewish history, theology and the Bible. We know that he gathered people around him, performed miracles, and was admired, feared and generally seen as a charismatic and extraordinary fellow--a grand, though mysterious, teacher and by some, a visitation of God on earth. Then the story tells us that he submitted himself to Pontius Pilate and was sent up to be crucified. He suffered three hours of pain on the cross, died, resurrected and three days later, appeared to his disciples.

Logic check. Christian doctrine says Jesus was fully man and fully god. Therefore he is omnipotent as well as being vulnerable. Which supersedes? The human being is human and also animal. Which supersedes? In the case of a person, his humanness supersedes (knowledge of future, conscious products, control of environs, etc.) over his animal nature. In the case of Jesus, his divine omnipotence supersedes. Does he feel pain? Only if he wants to--he's *omnipotent*. In that case, is it pain? No, because what we want to feel is called "pleasure", regardless of what someone else might feel in similar circumstances. His pain, your Gain? I think it is a case of the Winking Jesus again, fully in charge of the circumstances, as the evangelical Christian wants to be.

The believer in Pathological Christianity thinks he has cut a deal. He has been conditioned to think he is working a deal with God. I give homage, prayer, humility, accept God's presence in my life, therefore, I should feel better, do better, generally have a better life. Then perhaps things go to hell in my life. I get cancer, and cry out "Why Did This Happen To Me? I Was Good!" Egocentricity and entitlement follow on the heels of believing that there is A Plan, and that God's Will Is Good For His People. There is an answer in Pathological Christianity once a person is backed up to a Why Did This Happen To Me. This is the payoff for Pathological Conditioning. If things go badly for me, I simply must remember:

1. I have a personal relationship with Jesus and God
2. God never does me wrong, but gives me what I need
3. I either a)asked for the wrong thing b)asked in the wrong way

> if a) I need to pray for wisdom in order to ask for the right things

> if b) God was teaching me a lesson about attitude. I need an attitude adjustment.

- •*Pathological Christianity promotes grandiosity and entitlement*
  - • *The message to "Christians": you are "special" or unique because saved*
    - • This conditioning then has the dual effect of
      - a. making people stupid/ineffective
      - b. engendering an attitude of entitlement

Pathological Conditioning, the Nowlife and the Afterlife:
A Study in Irony and Political Rhetoric

Pathological Christians (especially the cheery Americans) have lost the essence of a strong, historical, traditional strain, perhaps the most basic root of Christianity. Christianity is about preparing for death and getting a place in heaven. The concern is not my life now, but life after death--the big Plan. Thus, I should have entirely no concern for my life now. I should not care a bit whether I have a dollar or not, whether I live in squalid circumstances or in a mansion, whether a Democrat or Republican is elected. Or if I do care, I should care only to the extent that it impedes the people around me in their detachment from the world and movement toward heaven. What should always be repulsive to me is anything that draws me to the world, draws me to acquisition, to obtaining, to becoming fixed on the things, persons or actions of this world, since my true concern needs to be the afterlife.

In this light, pain, chaos, disruption, dirt, sweat, sex, excitement, passion, terror, art and ideas are all bad because they interrupt or disrupt my continuous fantasy of certitude about heaven.

I should ignore everything of this world in order to focus all on dying well and going to the bosom of my Lord. This is what Jesus did. He did not concern himself with comfort, with acquisitions, wealth or good reputation. Jesus *was clearly against the comfortable family, as a distraction from higher things*, as we can see in his living model of how to act in the world.

However, in contrast to the model of Jesus,

- Pathological Christians are obsessed with *comfort and the good life*
- They are focused on controlling and politicking the world to make things good for Pathological Christians.
- They promote the view that your faith will get you comfort in the things of the world
- Attainment of comfort has actually become synonymous with godliness
- Pathological Christianity is *comfort-seeking* rather than *truth seeking*.

Idealization and Entitlement: Delusions of Grandeur in Pathological Christianity
[a crack in the person cracks the whole person]

Jerry

A "Christian lay preacher," writer, and speaker we will call "Jerry" has a "ministry" which has been very successful in its endeavors. Successful means that it is made a heap of money, gotten a large number of people to subscribe to its writings and sponsored events of grand drama and attendance at churches and auditoriums across the nation and even around the world, where many people have "come to the Lord." Jerry has hoarded many treasures as a result of some "fancy dancing" with words in books and "on stage." He's written several books on "Christian living" which have sold very well indeed. He is by all appearances living the American Dream.

Jerry's books and speeches portray a life of "happiness in the Lord." He and his wife Lois have two daughters, Angela and Christina. One of his books, *Father and Daughter*, is a book in which Jerry answers the questions his daughter Angela has had over the years about Jesus, the Bible, why people suffer and why *their* family is so happy when other families are so sad. *Father and Daughter* is Jerry's most admired book, seen by many as an outstanding and moving portrait of this difficult relationship filled with powerful and wise advice about family life and following the way of the Lord.

On his speaking tours, Jerry is inundated with requests to visit with "families in trouble," to pray with them for their recovery in the Lord, and to counsel them in Biblical principles to help get them back on the track of living a righteous life. He is admired for, as one woman put it, the "deep love he has for his family in Christ, and the way he leads us all by his example into the proper joining of family and the Lord."

Jerry's actual life is a dark shadow of this image, the Hyde to his public Jekyll. He lives in an upscale house in an upscale neighborhood and drives a new car, but what does he do? Most of his time at home is spent sleeping. He has never had much to do with his daughters, other than to rage at them occasionally and threaten them (using wild and graphic profanity) and sermonize at them about how they must guard their virginity and be "humble servants of God." He drinks profusely when awake, takes drugs prescribed by various doctors for factitious conditions; he has a stash of amphetamines which he uses during his speaking tours.

His wife Lois goes with him on his tours, and smiles sweetly when other people congratulate her on living with such a wonderful husband.   In reality, the two of them had no relationship as lovers or friends for at least ten years, though Jerry has had several affairs since the first year they were married through the present--though he has claimed to her that he was impotent.

Lois has been in therapy for many of those years and several times pressured Jerry to join her. The first psychologist they consulted confirmed Lois's belief that Jerry was truly addicted to at least three drugs and alcohol, and he refused to work with them unless Jerry dried out and got into a twelve-step program. He also confronted Lois for staying in the marriage and, in effect, giving approval to Jerry's behavior, paving the way for possible abuse of their daughters..   Jerry not only refused to get himself off drugs, but claimed the psychologist was an "idiot," and that since he questioned Lois for staying with him, the psychologist was obviously merely a "secular practitioner" and clearly did not understand "Biblical principles."

Jerry then consulted with a "Christian" psychiatrist (a man who had written Jerry in admiration of his writings), who instructed Lois that she just needed "to give Jerry more time," and told her that it was a wife's job to be a "servant leader" for her husband, to be patient and give of herself in prayer. The physician then gave Jerry several new prescriptions.

Although he was always blubbering about how "hard life is," how much "suffering" he had to do for other people, and that he'd "be better off dead," one night Jerry did overdose on drugs and was taken to a hospital where an alert young doctor got him in a three-day de-tox program. The psychiatrist that dealt with Jerry said that he was one of the "most narcissistic, delusional and uncooperative and downright nasty people" with whom he had ever come in contact.

Over the years, Jerry has made a great deal of his money through "contributions" from his many readers and supporters throughout the United States and abroad. In fact, his annual income from these contributions alone is well over fifty thousand dollars, though Lois suspects that it far in exceeds that. Nobody will ever know how much it is, because Jerry keeps very scant records, sheltering all income under the aegis of a "non-profit" organization called "Global Enterprise." Patrons and fans pour dollars his way following each "donation letter" he sends--full of high ideals, heart-rending stories and guilt barbs. Some of his financial supporters, ones who are close to Lois, even know the entire story of what actually happens at home. Why do they send money? Because they still "believe in him." Despite all he has done, he is still a "man of God."

Does this matter? Shouldn't his "message" be enough, without having to focus on whether the man lives up to it or not? No, because any "message" has to be powerful enough that it can actually deepen and strengthen the person who is supposedly living it. Idealization deadens, when it is a pretense that there are people who are actually embodiments of that idealization. Idealization kills, since it conditions us to believe that impossible goals can be achieved. It gives the fantasy that "you can do this," when in fact many of the things that are suggested by the Idealized are simply their own arbitrary fantasies of how to live.

Renee Lindsey

Renee tells her story:

"I come from possibly the most beloved and respected family in St. Charles, Missouri. My grandfather was a general in World War II, and personal friends with Eisenhower.   My grandmother was the founding president and for many years the chair of the Board of Directors of one of the largest children's hospitals in the world. My father invented or designed a lot of the more technical machinery used in mechanics shops today. He was a real genius. I say "was" because I think his mind has turned to mush now. Since he retired, he just mopes around the house. My mother--well my mother just *is*. She is a bigwig on just about every important social service organization in the county. She is the head of an international student exchange organization that emphasizes Christian principles. She was listed last year as one of the One Hundred Most Influential Women in America by some organization last year--I can't keep them all straight.

I am forty two years old. Up until the time I was forty, I lived at home. Not all the time, but I kept moving out and then moving back home. I have had several long-term relationships with men, but none of them was up to my mother's standards. I have a Master's Degree in Counseling, a teaching credential, speak five languages fluently and play piano very well. I've written for numerous magazines, done research for several prominent authors, taught university classes, traveled all over the world, and spent two years in Ecuador working at an evangelical mission, where I also stood in as a medical assistant, doing physicals, giving training to new mothers, occasionally helping with surgery.   In practical terms, I am probably as knowledgeable about medical matters as many nurses.

I don't mean to sound vain, but I am also fairly attractive. I did some modeling in my twenties, and have been compared in looks with Liv Ullman. It shocks me to even mention this, because until a couple of years ago I always pictured myself as loathsome, ugly, fat, stupid and yapping all the time. This is not to say that I have not determined myself to look beautiful or sound good to others--to the contrary! As my mother always would say, *We Lindseys may not be the most gifted people on earth, but by the grace of God, we do our best!*

My mother always uses the pronoun "we," assiduously avoiding "I". It's a way she has of communicating that *we* are a "family," even though it is *she* who makes all the decisions about what should be done, how each of us should dress, act, think and feel. She has also always had this habit of complimenting each person, continuously, in such a way that each time she compliments me I feel it is a way of correcting me.

I have a sister, Jane, who is three years older than I. She has really screwed up, according to my parents. She has not been a very good part of the "we." She got pregnant while in college, and made the mistake of telling mom and dad. They told her she'd just have the baby and move home for a while. My mother would have liked nothing better than to have another little child to save.. Jane decided to have amniocentesis to check out the baby's sex and found out that it was going to be mentally retarded, have the sex characteristics of male and female, and possibly be a giant with only little stubs of arms growing out from the shoulders.. She decided to have an abortion. My mother said to her, "I am going to say this just once--what you are doing is a sin. God will punish you, and I will always hold it against you. What God has offered you, you have refused. When God gives you a child, you take what he gives you."

That kid, despite being born with deformities, would have been somehow brought into being a "Lindsey," which is to say, being "perfect." I am not sure exactly how my mother might have accomplished this, but she would have. We were always "the perfect family." Whenever Reverend Pauling wanted to speak about family life, the very model of family life, he spoke of the *Lindseys*; whether he used our name or not, everyone knew he was speaking of us.

Since I was about twelve I have had a pretty blatant eating disorder; no, excuse me, it was absolutely obvious. I would be skinny as a rail for three months, but suddenly balloon out to 180 pounds, and I'm five feet seven inches tall. I would be rolling around the house like a globe of the earth with zits like a redwood forest all over my face, and then drop down to one hundred pounds and my hair would start falling out and my gums would bleed and my period stop, and *no one in my family, nor anyone in the church, nor any of the friends of my parents, nor even anyone my own age would ever say a thing about it.*

As I think of this now, I am really astonished, but somehow, the whole thing is perfectly clear and logical. The family could not see *individuals nor differences,* so no matter how much I weighed or how I looked, no matter how I was feeling, no matter what I did, my family could never see a thing. I myself hardly noticed any of these drastic changes. I kept my grades good, went to church every single Sunday, sang in choir, never came in late, and never let a boy lay a hand on me. I wonder now if some good sex might have knocked me out of my trance; God forbid I should say such a thing. As my mother would say, *Keep smiling, sweetheart, that Lindsey smile will wash away all your troubles.* We could never wear black or any other "gloomy colors," never be sad or openly laugh and as a family, we made fun of people who cried easily at a movie. It was *de rigor* to be disgusted at overt shows of emotion of any kind in public, other than a "fine and lovely and cheerful Christian smile, a *Lindsey smile*." I only recently thought about the fact that she wasn't after all a *Lindsey* herself by birth, but a *Klugenhoffer*.

I was always hoarding food, especially Snickers bars and such, all over the house. The odd thing, and something that only surfaced in my mind as odd in the last couple of years, believe it or not, was that I was always discovering food that *my mother* had hoarded all over the house herself. I'd just put it back when I found it, and she did the same. We actually caught each other numerous times, but went on about our business like zombies who had been trapped in some mental zone where thinking doesn't happen. It only floated up into my awareness that I was always *hearing my mother vomiting in the upstairs bathroom* on a daily basis. Nobody said a word about this.

Mom baked chocolate chip cookies every day of the year. All my friends came by the house and grabbed cookies, so it seemed understandable that they would all be gone each evening. But I just did some math and realized that five dozen cookies is *sixty* cookies. Not more than five or six kids came by each day after school, and let's say that each one ate *five each*. That still leaves about *thirty cookies*, and they would all be gone by the time my dad got home around six-thirty in the evening. They were not my food of choice, nor my sisters', so my mother had to be eating at least *two dozen cookies* every day of the year, yet she stayed quite thin and beautiful. She's still thin, though at age sixty-five her skin, hair, teeth and stomach have advanced in age beyond her years. I know the reason why.

In my Master's in Counseling program and in personal psychotherapy, I got quite a few shocks when we looked at family dynamics, secrets in the family, loyalties, and the all the processes that are used to keep things *status quo*, so that nothing can change. My family could not tolerate to be anything other than *the perfect Lindseys*, and I cannot begin to estimate the cost of that idealization for each and every one of us. I know I'll never be able to have the kind of closeness and frankness with my parents that I would like. I am far more sad about that than angry. I think my sister and I may be able to really become friends now that I have moved out on my own and have stopped protecting our parents from her. That sounds so strange to say, but I know it's true.

My father, since he retired, has done nothing but build up his Sunday school class. He now has the largest Sunday school class in St. Charles, in all of St. Charles, and he gears up for that and looks incredible on Sunday. The rest of the week all he does is drink, drag himself out of bed around noon, and play a little golf. He is the most depressed person I've ever met. But he always puts on the most lovely performance for the Sunday School. As I watch the two of them in their little cocoon, performing away, I get so sad and such a strange feeling comes over me. I know how utterly crazy and unnatural the whole little "perfect Christian" routine is. All I can say to anyone who might listen to me is don't let yourself get drowned in that poisonous way of living. For God's sake, no, for your children's sake, come out of this idealization, and let God and Jesus take care of themselves. I have a long way to go to get myself clear, but I am working on it, and though I face the future with uncertainty and fear without my blanket of "perfection" around me, I am feeling alive and real--like I have awakened from a very long, very deep sleep."

What is Idealization, And What Harm Can It Do?

Idealization is substituting an idea or a fantasy for an experience or direct perception. It is living according to some abstract principles of living rather than attempting to develop maturity in yourself as an individual and in your relationships with other people. How many times I have seen women or men in psychotherapy who have read books on self-development or magazine articles on "healing your relationship" trying to impose these fantasies on actual relationships. This is killing. There is a limit to the helpfulness of books or magazines focusing on "relationships." They deal in abstractions or fantasies, and create in the reader a false sense of knowledge. Women in particular seem prone to take magazine articles which feature such titles as "How to Heal Your Relationship," and "Getting the Love You Want From Person You Want It From," seriously.

The effects of idealization

- it abstracts or separates us from actually living life: we begin to live in romantic fantasies rather than in life
- eliminates your need or even desire to think or be in contact with other people
- causes you to seek another person's identity rather than your own
- confuses a person's manicured and carefully rehearsed persona with the entire person (actually many idealized people do this as well about themselves)
- forces you to *always find yourself lacking*, since a real life cannot be exemplary nor interesting at all times as you imagine some idealized person's life is.

Sara

Sara's father was a "deeply loved" minister/missionary in China, enormously popular. Her father once spoke to an audience of a almost a half-million people in a huge stadium.. "Everyone" saw him as one of the most magnificent people ever, and over the years he had become one of the most revered figures in the world of missionaries.

Sara knew her father only as the totally absent person, a man who never seemed to have even a single moment of time for any real conversation or love toward his own family, to his own personal development. All she knew of him as an emotional being was an occasional dirty look, a sermon delivered on sex, a lecture on discipline, a contrived beatific smile in front of the congregation, a person who paraded her private life in his sermons, generally a user of everyone's good will, money and time. She also knew that her mother had felt profoundly lonely all her adult life, since her father had never been "in" the marriage.

The Sources of Idealization

Idealization happens as a natural defense against the terrible truth that all human experience and all human solutions (including those which advise "leaving the world behind," "joining with the ultimate," "going beyond the mind," "moving into bliss beyond understanding" or other such nonsense) are just that: ordinary. The raw fact of life cannot be avoided, only delayed, ignored or handed to another for the fantasy of cure.

Idealization is an attempt to avoid naked or direct experience, to imagine that there are people or beings who can conquer or avoid life as such. In fact, such beings exist, but only on the cannibalism of other people, of followers who are willing to make life an opiate for their leader through idealizing him, giving him money, attention, love, admiration. Without the gullibility and service of followers, the leaders themselves would have to face all the raw experience that ordinary people do. What passes for spiritual advancement is in fact only psychological technology, the ability to induce trance in others to such an extent that the inductor himself is convinced of the illusion.

One might ask, what harm does idealization do? Don't people need heroes, fantasy figures to stir them on, to drive them to higher goals, to stimulate values?

Idealization: *forms of harm*

a) Individuals who are followers (idealizers) never reach any maturity themselves, but leave that to leaders (evangelists, etc.).

b) Evangelists and other leaders vampire their followers; very few people can resist the temptation to use their power to take things from those who admire them.

c) Evangelists themselves are deluded by their own trance, and become quagmired in their own hallucinations, thus themselves never reaching any maturity.

d) Entitlement fantasy is endlessly continued, because the leaders model some kind of "salvation" or "development" or "ultimate growth" which they do not possess, which does not exist, and which leaves people wanting, believing in, hoping for and believing they are entitled to at any cost to other people, the environment, the populous.

e) Needless wars, international conflicts and conflicts among family, friends and other people continue because idealization leads to rigidity, defensiveness, intolerance and hatred. Once a person has given up his individuality for a cause, and his investment of character, family, money and the like is done, is he likely to go back on this investment, and *look foolish?* Not likely.

f) In continuation of (e), where there is idealization, its opposite is always present as the "shadow." That is, where one thing, person or idea is idealized, other things, persons or ideas are *vilified.* When you vilify, you condemn. A person who is condemned is nothing, so it is no problem to hate and hurt that person, since he is no longer a person at all in the proper sense of the word. The only escape from hatred is to stop idealizing people, things or ideas.

Chapter 4. *Saviors and Babies: Pathological Christian Symbiosis*

PATHOLOGICAL CHRISTIANITY DIVIDES ALL humanity into Saviors and Babies, who live together in symbiosis. Symbiosis is a biological term referring to relationship of organisms which cannot live apart, but require one another for their survival.

Saviors are those who have some special gift, some special talent of "prophecy," "wisdom" or the like. Saviors are evangelists, leaders, CEO's of God's Company. Saviors are the darlings of Pathological Christianity, the privileged, sanctified ones. They are the bright twins of Catholicism's dark Saints, since they do not live on bread and vinegar nor die by thorns and inverted hangings, but live in sweet bungalows and have admirable haircuts and speedboats. Unlike a saint, the evangelist seeks not anonymity nor disappearing into Christ but stages for performances of his gig. He knows the *babies* will come, he knows their needs, their suckling gripes and ailments, and he knows the little song to sing to *make it all better.*

The *saviors* are reparenting their congregation. Now you have left your old birth, your old way, the way of living in a world of hurt, frustration, pain and death. You have come into the world of the new birth, a world of prayer, of God's help, of joy, triumph and the victory over death. Rejoice!

Saviors have technology. They have newsletters, they have advertising, they have psychological understanding of the deep longings and endless loneliness of the *babies*. They know how to tailgate on the forsaken, to offer them a bump up.

Saviors are the good parents, the long-fantasized parents, the parents you never had. They will offer you what your parents never could, since mom and dad were mere human beings. No, the *saviors* can offer something far superior to other mortals, they can show you how to get the *keys to the kingdom*. What the saviors can show you can make you washed clean, forever forgiven and unconditionally loved They have the technology to make you immortal and eternally felicitous. But beware, the path is narrow and many are the temptations, few are the ones who squeeze through (though all are invited, given they *conform*); but you, my friend, will be in that number. See how babies grow to feel entitled (as well as confused and ashamed)?

Who are the *babies,* and why do they believe this? Why do they give their souls up to this Pyramid Scheme? The *babies* are the unwashed masses, those who live trembling, waiting to be saved. Surely someone, Christ, Buddha or Santa Claus, will bring me the soothing I so *desperately need*, they think to themselves.

Pathological Christianity encourages, even **demands**, intellectual and emotional laziness and incompetence on the part of the many. Obey and be still is the command from the Judeo-Christian god, and he is not talking about meditative stillness but about "shutting up." When so many are obedient, things are just oh so much nicer in Centerville. Pathological Christianity finds great worth in the *babies* of all ages, and suggests *child likeness* as a route to heaven. "Be as the children, become like a child" is the motto offered to adult babies. Nowhere does the Pathological Christian message say, think and feel carefully and behave according to the highest level of your adult maturity, but rather, obey, be good, do as I say. Now, the *saviors* don't say really, do as *I* say, but do as the Lord says, which is a way of using God's name to shame *babies* into doing what they want them to do.

Steven, a fourteen year old kid with loads of intellect, curiosity and exuberance, dared to question his father, Ned, on several pronouncements the father made about certain political questions. Ned told Steven to be silent and that the boy had no right to question him, he'd consulted the Bible and his views accorded with the teachings of the church and good Christians. When Steven asked why he couldn't at least challenge his father, Ned told him that it was because he was the father, and the Good Book says Honor thy father and mother. Then he lectured him on "the family," on the ill morals of the country caused by children disobeying their parents. Steven knew that his father was powerless using this ploy. He had asked for a good reason and he liked to scuffle verbally with his father. His father was keeping him a *baby*, with the attitude that Steven had no right to exercise a perfectly good mind.

On that day, Steven knew he'd crossed the line between accepting his father's word for things and making up his own mind. If his father could do no better than a feeble excuse such as this, his views could hardly be worth much, Steven thought. Although he still loved his father, and would obey his house rules, Ned had lost his integrity on this day by hiding like a coward behind a principle rather than taking himself and his son seriously, admitting that his view was merely his own belief, and encouraging the son to make up his own mind. Fortunately Steven had the good sense to decide to grow toward his own autonomy rather than be diminished by this kind of talk from his father.

The famous Swiss psychiatrist Carl Jung tells in his autobiography *Memories, Dreams, Reflections* of a couple of similar moments in his life. The first was when his father, a Lutheran pastor, refused to discuss the concept of the Trinity with young and inquisitive Carl, but sheepishly lowered his head and kept silent. Another such incident happened when Jung and Freud were crossing the Atlantic to deliver a series of famous lectures on the new field of psychoanalysis in America. Freud was the elder, and Jung was something of an apprentice in those days, though he was already in his thirties a precocious President of the Psychoanalytic Society.

Along the way, the two of them discussed theories and views about the practice of psychoanalysis. In the conversation, Jung tells Freud a few dreams, which Freud interprets profusely. One day, Jung tells his elder that he appreciates the thoughtful interpretations, but asks Freud why he does not tell some dreams. Freud says, "But I cannot risk my authority!" From that day forward, Jung recognized that there was a profound flaw in Freud's approach, which did not allow him the courage to speak freely and openly with a colleague about himself, but to guard some position of idealization and "authority."

Sadly, it is hardly any better state of affairs with most psychotherapists today, let alone pastors or others in positions of "authority." One might think that psychotherapists would be a group particularly open to the "risk" of being seen as ordinary human beings, as people with the same kinds of worries, sufferings and confusions as everyone else, with the possible difference of their attitude of courage, integrity and straightforwardness about revealing this ordinariness. Alas, many therapists have bought the vision of the "healer," some view of themselves as better than, superior to or different from any other person. Such crazy notions are juiced up by the uproarious and childish images of suburban college-educated people who can't tell a mulberry from a whippoorwill suddenly hallucinating that they are *tribal shamans* or that thumping on a drum or having a few fetishes in their 12th street office makes them Stone Age medicine persons.

Many therapists of the New Age ilk thus themselves have fallen (exactly like their "Christian Counselor" colleagues) into the darkest and most harmful condition that their profession encourages people to avoid--the pit of hypocrisy and "image-making," as opposed to direct and gutsy living. They are "playing it safe," not risking their authority. They offer themselves up as a model of a person who has "arrived" at some psychological or spiritual height and is a more "evolved" person, and thus offer their elevated status as a healing role model for people less advanced. *There are no such people.*

The <u>true</u> power of psychotherapy comes in its strength to *erode* people's certainty, rigidity and fantasies of themselves, and force them to recognize that they are just ordinary people, and that illusions and fantasies keep us from having real feelings and thoughts.

A Little Parable from a psychotherapy session, and from the story of Don Quixote:

> *A patient says to her therapist after one session, "I can't tell you how much better things are between my husband and me since our session. It is unbelievable, wow! It is truly a miracle. By the way, we are going to have to cancel our session for Wednesday, since Ray is going to be out of town. I will call you sometime to reschedule. Again, thanks so much, it seems like a miracle." And how long will this miracle endure, the hard-working therapist asks himself? As long as I can still imagine I have made a miracle, he answers. But when I leave the scene?*

> *Don Quixote was ambling on his way to do noble and chivalrous deeds in the world, riding on his exhausted nag Rocinante and wearing a barber's basin for a helmet. He came upon a road gang, who had been fixing some stone work on a retaining wall. The prisoners working on the gang had been worked to total depletion. The guards were convinced the prisoners were slacking, and were beating them ferociously.*

Quixote dismounted and threw himself between the guards and the prisoners, announced in noble tones who he was, and demanded that the guards stop cudgeling the prisoners with their clubs and whips. The guards bowed to him and (winking at each other) said that they would obey His Grace, and that they begged his pardon.   Quixote nobly gave a nod and admonished the guards, then mounted his miserable nag and strode on, properly proud of his deed.   Once he had rounded the corner, the guards commenced whipping the prisoners with twice the fury they had before Quixote came along, as payment for interruption of their work.

Fantasy of the Absolute Parent

An evangelist tries to be the *absolute* parent, absolute in the sense that he needn't punish wrongdoings nor give praise, support, or love his children. He has God behind him and *God* does it all for him. He only need speak the term and the overweening power of the Almighty is upon the *babies*, the children of his "ministry."   How odd the term *minister*, which means to serve or servant, when the *babies* are the ones who serve the evangelist. A better term would be *autominister*, which would mean "self-serving."

The *autominister* thus could join the work force just where he belongs, in the long, bleak row of retail businesses in the *strip mall.* His services could rightly join those of the drive in hamburger joint, the self-serve gas station, the convenience mart, the self-storage garages, the automated electronic tellers, and his messages could be encrypted on the code readout bar-strip on each retail product. We could have little scan guns for our Bibles, with electrodes hooked to the head which would then drive home a little electronic spurt to a particular recess of the brain, reminding us to *trust only the born again Christian, vote conservative, picket abortion clinics, disavow feminists, pray for democracy and keep our women pregnant for Christ,* giving us little shocks, or great big ones, if we are tempted to transgress. Autoministers would have the little recharging units for the scan guns, and would program them, and we'd have less crime, or art, or nasty people or people who aren't just like us running around the streets. Praise be to Jesus!

Conversion Experience
or
How to Become a Baby in One Easy Lesson

- Convert. You will be an entirely new, different, higher, better you. All you have to do is accept Jesus [or something] into your life.
- It will happen by this formula or incantation that you'll release all the bad and get a magic infusion of all the good.
- You'll be born again, washed clean (though your body is still a tissue of sin, and must be monitored and controlled by Jesus, since you can't do it.)
- Remember this: nothing is symbolic in Christianity. All is real, literal, historical. Don't forget!
- Don't think, feel or act without praying first, so that the Holy One can guide you. *You wouldn't want to make a mistake, would you? Remember, one mistake can poison a whole life forever!*
- When you come over to the right side of the tracks, not a speck remains of your former life. You are brand new.
  "Conversion" is the <u>con-version</u>

Saviors and Babies: a Corrective

The only honest position for a minister, counselor, healer or for any human being with another is to say, "I have no answers for you in your life, there is no way for me to know what is right for you. I can only help you hear what you say and help you reflect on what you do, from which you must draw your own conclusions. I must take care of my own life in the meanwhile, though I will serve you in ways that don't diminish my soul or make either of us the slave of the other.. If you try to use my conclusions about how to live, I might be tempted to feel flattered and puffed up, and then I will not see you as an equal, but as an inferior. I am not your *savior* and you are not a *baby*. I can make one hypothesis, however, that in the end anyone will be much happier thinking for oneself, though getting used to such practice takes time and can be a real killer."

Theological Codependency
Roots of so-called "codependency": God as "Alcoholic Father"

A trend in popular psychology in recent years has been to adopt into general vocabulary, terms or descriptions from either slang or other understandings in non-psychological settings, such as business, legal affairs, politics or, in the case at hand, the group Alcoholics Anonymous, a social control movement which uses paradox and rigid guidance to get people to quit booze and stay off the stuff.

The paradoxical part of AA (and other so-called twelve step programs) is that they say, go ahead and live your life, we can't stop you from drinking (or other harmful acts), but when you are ready, then we'll tell you how to run every detail of your life. Come in and freely give up your freedom. An intriguing concept, but certainly you can see that it's once again Pathological Christianity with a little different slant, the fake image of acceptance of bad behavior, the tricky attitude of acceptance of people "how they are." I say it is fake, because AA is actually Pathological Christianity with a little more patience. *The bums will fall on their butt and die doing so or they will eventually come around to the right way,* is the basic premise.

One of the terms adopted by popular psychology from AA is "co-dependent." The original meaning came from the view that an addict is *dependent* on his substance of choice, while those around him get high by letting him get high and not having him arrested, kicking him out or abandoning him. The *high* garnered by the "co-dependent" is that she gets to feel like she's a *good person* because she believes in a jerk who *at heart, is really a good guy.* Her high is the electricity that comes from telling lies, which always has some sense of excitement. Sometimes, she gets herself beaten up also, physically or verbally, which is a kind of spanking she thinks she deserves-- another form of high. Kids and adults brought up in an environment of Pathological Christianity always think they deserve a spanking or beating, because they believe they are irredeemably bad, guilty, naughty and sinful. Oddly enough, it gives people a buzz to feel terrible, tortured and submitted to someone cruel and arbitrary, like for example a mean alcoholic father or husband.

Pathological Christianity teaches us to get saved from ourselves, by submitting ourselves to something higher, mightier, better, richer, and forever more right than we can ever be about

ourselves.   It's term for this something we are to submit
ourselves to is *God.* But in many ways it seems that there are
striking similarities between this God and an "alcoholic father,"
as defined by the current "recovery" literature. My purpose in
making this analogy is to uncover the roots of psychological disease, and demonstrate that these roots dig far deeper than
problems with alcohol or even current confusions about families,
but extend to the very essence of our assumptions about
humans, the world, the universe and the Creator. Also, I wish to
explain why Pathological Christianity can never hold the keys for
satisfaction for us as individuals or members of a family, and
why we will always feel inferior, guilty and crazy under the sway
of Pathological Christianity.

What kind of image do we get of God as he is portrayed
in the Bible? Like an "alcoholic father," he is often absent,
arbitrary and jealous, explosively sensitive to criticism. He is
here and than gone. One moment he is speaking with strength
and power to his children and then he seems to disappear for an
undisclosed amount of time, during which we are supposed to be
convinced that he loves us despite his long silences and
absences.

God, like many alcoholic fathers, punishes his children
suddenly, swiftly and intensely. He gives and takes away. He
brings his first born children into a Paradise, the most beautiful
place that has ever existed, a wonderful home full of stunning
curiosities and magnificence, but then banishes and exiles them
forever into eternal punishment (especially women, who are
condemned to the pain of childbirth) for disobeying an absurd
and unreasonable, arbitrary command that he gives, a command
that human beings could never follow, that is, to resist eating
from the Tree of Knowledge. Pathological Christianity reveals
its hand when it portrays the primary sin of humans as curiosity,

the desire to know and explore and be conscious. The alcoholic father cannot be contested, he cannot bear challenge or even the existence of competition to his position of absolute authority. It has always struck me odd that an omniscient, omnipotent God would feel threatened by plain human beings having a moiety of consciousness. The story clearly has more to do with political power and the power of men over women and children than it does with some deeply loving deity.

It is common knowledge that drunk fathers have wildly shifting moods, which seem to come and go without reason or explanation, and that this is the attribute that most dismays and frightens children. Children simply do not know how to act or how to be in order to "please daddy," make him "feel better" and thus avoid the consequences of his erratic moods. One moment he is cold and fierce dispensing "justice" all over the place, punishing and whipping the family into shape, criticizing everybody in sight. Then next moment he is sappy, sentimental, whimpering and blubbering all over everybody, telling them he loves them, that he is sorry about his harshness, that he asks their forgiveness. Though God is rarely portrayed in whimpering and blubbering imagery, he is often shifting in imagery between a zealous, fierce being who can destroy almost every being on earth, including innocent animals, in the Flood, when he perceives their disloyalty to him; then he is one who loves and calls his children to him seen as "merciful," "loving," the tenderest protector and Creator. We know that children feel or even become crazy under the kind of wild oscillation in feeling and action that happens in alcoholic families--the evidence is clear. What has not been so clear is that the whole of Western Civilization has been living under a similarly arbitrary and "crazy-making" way of perceiving self and world.

One of the things that sons in particular have to suffer with their fathers in recent times is that the fathers want to say they care, or they communicate to someone (usually the mother) that they care but in the final analysis, the father doesn't "show up" for his son. He doesn't show his purportedly deep love by doing the most minimal efforts to demonstrate it. He makes work more important, playing golf, being with his pals, going out drinking, fiddling around in his workshop but not showing direct attention to a son or daughter who requires proof that he cares.

Jim, a seventeen year old high schooler with a real talent for tennis, describes something which will ring familiar in its essence to many people:

My mother is always saying, "You just have to understand that your dad loves you, he just doesn't know how to show it." But I have to tell you it seems more like I am in his way than someone he loves. He has only been to one of my tennis matches in two years, and I am ranked fourth in the state. Even when he came, he acted bored. When I finished I headed for the stands to talk to him, but he was already gone. I think he just came because my mother pressured him. He comes home late at night and leaves early in the morning, and is gone a lot of weekends on business. When he is at home, he's drunk. I try to talk to him when I see him, ask him how's it going and things like that, and he keeps saying he will take me out hunting or we'll go to an NFL game, but we never do. Every once in a while he leaves some money in my room or gets me a really nice present, like a motorcycle. I am not complaining about these gifts, and I appreciate them, but it is like I get them from a stranger. I don't even know the guy, so how can I take my mother seriously when she keeps saying things like, "He loves you, you just have to believe me and trust what I say, one day you will understand." I am beyond being angry about the whole thing. All I'm going to do is try not to depend on him. Maybe some day he will wake up and know that he needed to be more direct with me, not just keep me guessing or interpreting some vague or symbolic signs that he loves me or even thinks of me. All I know is that my children will deserve and get better.

It is the same way with the Biblical God. He says he cares--we have reports that he says he cares--but doesn't show up. Every once in a while he speaks to some prophet or other, who then tells the rest of us that God loves us. We are supposed to take it on "faith" that he cares, that he is always with us, that he is looking out for our best interest, that he takes an active concern and participation in our inner and outer lives. Perhaps these things are true, but in order for us to humanly respond, to sanely and reasonably accept such arguments, we would require much a more direct, intelligible and compassionate presence of a God or Creator. To give up our thinking, feeling and autonomous action on the basis of such obtuse, desperate and obviously political explanations is crazy, self-destructive, and infantile.

We know that the most loving and effective parents are those who can provide gentle but firm guidance while the child is very young, but gradually and conscientiously let go of their control over the child as he grows to adulthood. The hierarchy in successful families is one which shifts from the parents being in charge of their children when they are small and then later, shifting the scale to understanding, power and respect when the child moves into peer status as an adult among adults. We might think of the measure of successful parenting precisely as this: when the children become adults, there is no longer a power struggle between parents and children, but mutual respect. Gone will be lectures, sermons and attempts at guidance. In its place will be a friendship between equals in which parenthood in essence has disappeared, having already served its purpose.

This is not to say that parents and their children will no longer have many feelings, urges, wishes or longings, that were present when the children were young. A mother will always have certain feelings toward a person she bore in her womb, and a child always a certain residual feeling of some uncertainty or stored feeling toward parents. In terms of action, dialogue and demonstrated respect, however, an adult parent and child relationship that is the result of good parenting will have the following as its hallmark:

- the parents will not offer guidance but friendship, and will not pull "one-upsmanship"
- the children will only seek the kind of guidance from parents they might seek from friends
- parents and children will think of each other as fellow travelers in human life

Another difficult thing for many parents to do is to relinquish their requirements for loyalty and demonstrations of faithfulness on the part of children, to graciously let them go on about their own lives. This does not mean ignoring their grown children at all, but rather respectfully and warmly keeping the invitation to visit and spend time together as an offering of friendship, good will and interest rather than one of obligation, compunction or shame. People who are secure in themselves do not demand *constant* proofs of other people of their loyalty, though when people care deeply, they naturally and spontaneously give these "proofs." Some parents show obsession or jealousy if their children show more interest in other adults or their friends than they do in the parents themselves.

The Pathological Christian model for this is the "zealous god." God speaks saying "Thou shalt have no other gods before me." When this is uttered as a command, it naturally communicates a lack of self-confidence, the kind of petty, controlling attitude often held by adolescent boys and girls (and their parents) of their friends. Apparently the Biblical God is jealous you'll like somebody else better, and lacks the confidence you'll wish to keep him as a friend, or will remain loyal to him out of love or interest. He feels the need to demand loyalty (with all the implied punishments), in precisely the way that drunk fathers do when they are feeling sappy, sentimental and lost to themselves and to their world, alienated and afraid that no one will like them because they have been so nasty to everyone.

Another trait of alcoholic parents, alluded to already, is that they are *unreadable, except by a form of mind reading or anticipating of needs.* Profuse quantities of alcohol, drugs or Pathological Christianity cloud the mind and the thinking, but do not blunt the sting of need and demand for proofs of loyalty. Thus, through the haze of a trance, intoxicated parents oblige their children to serve them and soothe them, but do not give them adequate instructions on what precisely they must do. Children in such families must guess or make random attempts to do the right thing to calm and pacify their parents. Parents model and train their children to exhibit traits of narcissism in such circumstances, particularly the expectation of entitlement, that *someone* outside of themselves must make them *feel good, right, valuable, satisfied,* and the "someone" who is most tractable and most available is their children.

These parents learned from their parents who learned from a *narcissistic god* to expect children and others in relationship to "read between the lines," to "guess" at what they must do to satisfy the wounded and narcissistic parent. In a perverse way, it becomes the child's and/or the spouse's job to anticipate or guess the need of the alcoholic parent, and to do their best to satisfy the needs of that parent, in order to quell and soothe his hurts.

Additionally, the *narcissistic god* requires love and adoration without criticism. One must never criticize the God and mean it. A Pathological Christian may *temporarily* be angry or frustrated with God, because there is some recognition of inevitable human error, but he must quickly apologize and realize that he was quite mistaken, that the God could never really do something harmful or negative or wrong. In exactly the same way, one must never truly *challenge* the alcoholic parent, since it will wound him or her, and further, the consequences could be drastic and painful for one who criticizes. Let me explain.

The narcissist above all else cannot tolerate criticism, and will react quite disproportionately abusive of self or others in response to it. The reaction is way out of measure, and will either be one of rage and intense counter attack or a strong withdrawal and collapse. As you will remember, the narcissist feels empty and almost non-existent inside, and depends entirely on the external world to provide definition of his worth and sense of reality. Thus, a seemingly harmless criticism can *shatter* the world of the narcissist, since he depends entirely on praise to build existence and substance for himself. He will thus either feel quite crushed by criticism or take desperate measures to defend against it, by counter-attacking and vehemently refusing even the most benign criticism. He must constantly be built up, so he is constantly on guard against disloyalties or inattention to him. He says, in effect, *thou shalt have no other gods before me*, aping the zealous narcissistic God of the Bible.

The Biblical God requires of you, according to Pathological Christianity, that you give to him eternally. He requires an addictive level of attention from his children--and that they *ignore all his faults, take all problems or misfortunes or sufferings as wonderful demonstrations of his grace and glory and emphasize and praise endlessly his successes.* This is indeed a diagnostic portrait of the child abuser, the adult who uses children to gather power to himself and to cover his own lack of confidence. He (or, as we are finding more and more, *she*) requires proofs of loyalty from his children, regardless of his behavior. Right or wrong, hurtful or nurturing, he demands that each and every one of his acts be seen as righteous, good, the *right thing at the right time* for all concerned.

Since he is so disabled by criticism, he uses many maneuvers to avoid receiving it. One of these maneuvers is to send other people out to do the dirty work for him, so that he will remain removed from negative consequences. Alcoholic parents often require their children to protect them and their image. When the police come on the reports of neighbors that yelling and violence is taking place next door, the wife and the children are well trained to inform the police that "nothing is wrong." His wife, daughter or son guards his image and takes the punishment.

In effect, the Biblical God does the same thing with his son, Jesus. He sends his son out to do his dirty work, to clear his name and do public relations work for him, to convince people to believe in him. Jesus must go so far as to get humiliated, scourged and even killed while professing total loyalty to his father to impress potential followers with his dedication. I must admit that as I write this, I feel somewhere in my personality that I will be punished for my "disloyalty" to God, for daring to speak up against him and even for "exposing" what seems like a truth and a secret about him and about the way he behaves. It is incredible the extent to which such thinking permeates us.

In families of an alcoholic father, we often see that children and adult women are "frozen out" of the main business of making decisions. They have the obligation of maintaining the family and of keeping the daily affairs going, but when it comes to a decision by the father about any major or minor issue, the rest of the family members must be willing to go along. If the father it is crucial, however arbitrary it is in actual fact. Pathological Christianity supports entirely and consistently supports such patriarchal arbitrariness and diminishment of women and children.

I listened with incredulity to a nationally syndicated radio program (with millions of listeners) recently in which two evangelists were talking about areas in which a man should be willing to "negotiate" and not negotiate with the other members of his family. As an example of permissible "negotiation," they cited an example of a man who was being transferred to another town in his job. They said he should listen to the concerns of other members of the family and discuss these with them, before he makes up his mind. It is clear that when he makes up his mind, the decision must be Law. Their example of when he should never "negotiate" with his family was if a seventeen year old son decides he doesn't want to go to church some Sunday. They said that the father should simply state, "we are a family that goes to church, and you will too." Though the program was about "negotiation," it was clear that the entire concept had eluded them and that they had no clue about such activities as "discussion," "dialogue," or other such basic communication transaction, let alone the rather sophisticated (for them) process of negotiation.

Pathological Christianity, with its emphasis on control, guidance, hierarchies, power and guilt, will naturally not encourage such relationships to develop. Its goal is to make babies and keep them babies.

So, by way of summary, the features that prove similar between the God of Pathological Christianity (the prototype) and the alcoholic and narcissistic parent include:

- The "absent father" who is here, then gone, on his own schedule, according to his needs.
- He punishes and loves arbitrarily, apparently at his whim, confusing those who try to relate with him.
- He is cold and vengeful in one moment, then sappy and regretful and making new promises in the next; children do not know whom they are to trust or what it is that they are to trust about him.
- He says he cares but doesn't show up.
- He is self-obsessed, jealous and punishing if you like anybody else; doesn't allow his children to explore and like whom they wish to like; guards them for himself.
- He demands absolute loyalty in thought, word and deed, and punishes even the slightest indication of disloyalty.
- He is unavailable except by "reading the message" or "reading between the lines."

Narcissistic God: requires love and total adoration without criticism, sublimely and vehemently reactive to criticism or even the mention of existence of other deities.
- Sends his son out to do his dirty work
- Women and children are frozen out of the real business, yet are supposed to be there waiting.

- He requires that you give to him without proof of reciprocity: once every two thousand years or so he sends someone around to prove he exists.

This God requires an addictive attention from his children, that they ignore all his faults, take all problems as wonderful demonstrations of his grace and glory and emphasize and praise endlessly his successes.

Further, if you are his child, you do not need "consciousness"--as a matter of fact, the knowledge of good and evil is a sin, as is any form of thinking for yourself. Apparently this god, just like an alcoholic, cannot stand to be confronted and will act out his vengeance entirely out of proportion to the act if he so wishes. What kind of model is it to people that a god would create a paradise and then expel his children from it for an act of enjoyment or pleasure, such as eating from a tree out of curiosity? What kind of parent is this anyway? He is portrayed as arbitrary, jealous, spiteful, and capable of holding a grudge against the entire human race forevermore as the result of a quite innocent simple act on the part of one couple.

According to this, if you are a child, you need not have consciousness, The god is our consciousness, our parent. His co-parent, according to Pathological Christianity is the evangelical.

Chapter 5. *Family Pathology: The Pathological Model of the Holy Family*

RECENTLY CERTAIN PILOTS of Pathological Christianity have wrung their hands and spilt a great deal of ink over something they call *the family*. The essence of their angst can be summarized simply. There once was this exquisite thing called *the family* (or better yet, the *Christian family).* It was the vessel in which all the good things of the society were forged (along with another thing we will discuss later, the *Church*). People learned to be moral, correct, courteous, kind, godly, reverent, brave, thrifty, cheerful and clean in the family. Things were going along just great, at least in big, wonderful America, because God had invented this marvelous fortress of goodness which was being practiced properly here in the U.S. of A. Then something happened, blame it on the Sixties or drugs or whatever, but *the family began falling apart*. When this started happening, everything began to go bad. This, of course, is ironic. It is not really bad in ecclesiastical terms for things to go wrong, since the worse it is, the swifter comes the apocalypse predicted by Pathological Christianity, the sooner the chaff and the wheat are sorted and the sooner we are all in Heaven or Hell. Nonetheless, it seems to be important to try to get things straightened out in the meantime, particularly in order to recruit new inductees into the *Heaven Plan*.

At this era in our grand endeavor to follow God's Plan, we have slipped and slid into a moral abyss, into "godlessness." We must recapture what they refer to as the "traditional family" or "traditional family values." We must change back so as not to bring about the disappearance of Christianity. Many religions have come and gone in human history. Since Christianity is in its last gasp at least in its historical form, Pathological Christianity has come about as a reactive attempt to salvage the dying beast. The central motif in the Crucifixion is *The Comeback Kid*, so just because things are dark for the Christians does not mean that they are sad or down. Au contraire, they are ecstatic about the challenge. They love it when things look dark and desperate, since they can play *Saviors and Babies,* their favorite game.

There is strong evidence that we are evolving into really new definitions of "family," rather than rigidly continuing any fixed traditions. There is less and less respect for and blind acceptance of The Plan. This threatens Pathological Christianity to the bones. Christianity is a religion which rises and falls entirely on a gamble, that is that the whole universe is under the ultimate direction and control of its God, and that certain events have unfolded and will occur as scheduled. The survival of Pathological Christianity as a historical institutions depends on whether folks can be convinced that there is a specific, dogmatic and inevitable Script written for human history which results in salvation for the good believers and damnation for the rest of the chaff.

FANTASIES OF "THE FAMILY"

*The **family** is not **falling apart** because of **moral decay.** It is <u>changing</u>, and we are having a tough time knowing how to live with the changes. This thing called "the family" is and will always be in a state of flux and change. There is no use trying to inflict some idealization on "the family" about what it should look like. Like any human institution or activity, "the family" will constantly be evolving.*

Pathological Christianity teaches that you must seize radical change by the throat and squeeze all life out of it, in order to preserve what is correct and right and "godly" otherwise the evil force of the wickedness will come through and infect us all.   One form of this throat-squeezing is holding some cherished form of "the family" as sanctified, innate and immutable, and acting as if all other social forms are at best wrong minded or dirty, and at worst, depraved and perverse.

A little historical review of human existence shows that the family has taken on wide variation. "The family" has meant everything from the little insular nuclear triad of mom, dad and baby to a conglomerate of relatives responsible for child care, homecare and survival needs and even to societies in which the biological parents have very little to do with the upbringing of the children, since they are considered to be too biased. It does little good to rehearse anthropological or historical evidence of the permutations of the family to Pathological Christians, since their moral superiority simply dismisses anything outside of a recently formulated American social model taken somehow to be God's ideal ancient prototype for how people should be together. Lack of history and ignorance in general are the surest ways to preserve a sense of certainty and importance of what one believes.

So what we will do instead is to look at what ought surely to qualify in Christianity as the ultimate model of the family, that is the family of Jesus of Nazareth.   Surely no Christian would dare dispute the sanctity of the family of Jesus nor question the Holy Family's actions as the categorical prototype for the "traditional family." If we are to be Christians, which means Christ-like, we would attempt to follow the model in each thing and if evangelists wish for a model of the traditional family, what better source than Scripture for our standard, particularly when we have a direct exemplar in Jesus' own family?

Evangelicals are forever insisting that the Bible is the literal word of God given to us for our edification. So if we wish to take the Holy Family as a literal model for family, the things we wish to understand about the family by looking at Jesus *et famille* are a)the practice of marriage; b)childrearing practices; c)developmental psychology of children; d)parental attitudes; e) the child's attitude toward parents; f)guidance given to adolescents through those painful years of moving into adulthood. Since Pathological Christianity places so much emphasis on direct guidance from the Bible and rule following, let us see what can be done to follow the lead of the Holy Family in instituting what is called the "traditional family."

a) *The Practice of Marriage*

Mary was pregnant out of wedlock

She claims God did it. But even if God did "do it," why couldn't he wait until Joseph and Mary were married? This would have made Joseph a married cuckold rather than simply a cuckolded boyfriend. Could God not have explained directly to Joseph himself what was happening? Wasn't God man enough to face Joseph? Couldn't he have been pal enough to at least let Joseph in on the deal a little? Apparently not, so we have a model for out of wedlock sex, cuckolding, secrecy, mystery and a pact between God and women (involving impregnation and jealousy) that excludes men. Perhaps this is why Christianity has always had more women than men adherents and practicers, yet the hierarchy in the autoministry has always been male--after God, who gets the gal.

Did Mary and Joseph ever get married? There is no unchallengeable reference to this in the Bible. Therefore, we can assume from the model of the Holy Family that contrary to the ravings of the evangelicals, God smiles on unmarriage. Well, at least as long as he is the daddy. Might this confusion be part of the difficulty we have in taking marriage seriously, rather than the insistence that drugs or television or such are the cause of the problem? Perhaps we have become more irreverent toward such institutions as marriage, since *irreverence is modeled in the Holy Family.* People used to get married and stay married. Why? The reasons for this are not just reducible to some evangelical's whining reply that the world is going to hell. People stayed married in grand part because they were agrarian, economically bound and afraid of the wrath of the priests. Farm communities provided few opportunities for people to meet others, to form alliances outside of the immediate family and were extremely demanding physically and closed minded. Until recently, women were property of men--sexually, politically and economically--and so were trapped like caged rabbits, without rights or power to raise hell. They had no way of challenging the assumptions and political conclusions of Pathological Christianity about the dominance and control of men. This is why feminism is such a crisis for evangelicals: it threatens to upset the entire system of domination of *saviors,* who see themselves as stand-ins for God, having the right and franchise to pick out whatever virgin they wish to have the holy privilege of bearing their seed.

If we look at the Divine Menage A Trois, God-Mary-Joseph, we can see that as long as God is involved, relational trusts can be broken to suit the whim of the Divine One. Is the story of God's choosing Mary without discussing it with her an exemplary source from which some men draw the casual assumption that women are to be had at the whim of superior male power, or was the story written to accommodate male desire for dominance? According to some historians (this is controversial), a similar practice to God's intervention with Mary was carried on entirely here on earth. In some European countries, the Lord of the Manor or other nobility who ruled over a territory practiced the Right of First Night, in which a

virgin who was about to be married was deflowered by the
nobleman. It was considered his right to pick this first fruit of
womanhood. One wonders if one Western source of the
concept of this privilege, and of the nearly universal male
obsession with intercourse with virgins is not in the mythology
of God's harvesting Mary under the nose of Joseph.

Now mythology or storytelling is really just people
reflecting in interesting and profound dramas what they
experience on earth; perhaps there is some divine spark or
inspiration that takes place. In essence, myths such as the
impregnation of Mary may be less an object lesson in "this is
how it is done, do it like the gods," than a reflection in divine
imagery of the way things happen symbolically with human
beings all the time. I have given a feminist politic above about
the male hierarchical, so called "patriarchal" purpose of Biblical
literature; an evangelist or other faithful follower will show
another reading of the same story to try to get people to behave
how he feels they should. When you "draw a lesson" from a
divine story, you become a politician, whether feminist, Christian
or StoneWorshipper, and thereby turn what is a psychological
story of the complexity of the human soul into the current
Sunday School Lesson.

Our current theme is marriage. When we look at the
model for marriage in the Holy Family, we have to stretch our
imaginations and become quite brittle about our faith in order to
see much *in the exemplar of Joseph and Mary*, or in the life of
Jesus that gives us concrete instruction. That evangelizer Paul
later made relentless opinions out of his own interpretation that
have been taken as Christian, but if we disregard Paul as only a
mixed up chap and look at our real hero Jesus and his family, we
get a story that is clearly totally symbolic. My point is to
demonstrate that any time you look with a little amazement and

open-mindedness on well-conceived stories, you should get more confused, not less. The story of Jesus does **not** provide us with answers about how to solve the outer problems of life, what kind of family is right, what kind of childrearing practices are right, or any other external question. The story of Jesus actually provides us with an attitude, an attitude of openness, not answers to daily problems.

b) Childrearing Practices

What does the Holy Family demonstrate about childrearing practices? From the birth of Jesus, he is seen as a marvel, a strange wonder, a beautiful vulnerability who is arriving into a world of threat and danger. His parents' job is to worship him and protect him, to keep him from death, and *that's about it.* We hear no more in the Gospels about discipline, how to talk with kids about sex, expectations about grades in school, curfews, not another thing is modeled for us about how to bring up kids. When Autoministers admonish and exhort in lurid emotional tones about Christian upbringing and the like, look to the Holy Family. We see nothing there about "how to do it." The best we can do is infer from what we see about how Jesus was brought up, other than that his family was Jewish. Christian kids everywhere have been confused for two thousand years about how to be Christ-ian if they are not brought up Jewish. Perhaps this is one source of anger and frustration by Christians toward Jews, since they are actually brought up Jewish--like Jesus.

c) developmental psychology of children

What do we see about the development of children as modeled in Jesus? We must, perhaps, exclude the Gnostic gospels, such as the Gospel of Thomas and other "fringe" documents, which do have certain assertions about Jesus's childhood, and focus on the "standard" or "politically accepted"

Bible as it currently stands in Pathological Christianity. Again, we find very little indeed about the details of the child Jesus. As a baby we know that he was richly adored and proclaimed, a magnified (though sometimes not much) version of the attitude that most parents, relatives and friends have toward a newborn. It sometimes seems that the uglier the infant, the more people swoon. There is something in us that worships new birth and the new birth of Jesus is a richly ornamented story about this.

Yet we hear nothing about boy Jesus again until he is twelve and wowing them in the temple with his understanding of the prophets and their messages, making innuendoes and claims about his destiny and the like. Again, we can do little but infer (or consult other "heretical" sources) what happened meanwhile, but the ordinary years must have passed between infancy and twelve years of age and then twixt there and the turn of his thirtieth when he set out on his teaching sojourn.

d) parental attitudes, place of mother & father with children and with each other; child's attitude toward parents

The clearest statement of attitude of parent toward child is that by Mary of her son. She adores and worships him and makes herself his servant. The best we can tell, Joseph merely endures the existence of Jesus and at worst, sees him as a living symbol of his own hurt ego, since Jesus is the bodily reminder of his cuckolding. It doesn't matter whether the cuckolder happens to be God--as a matter of fact that part of the story seems to smell fishy to Joseph at best. Is he ever convinced that Jesus is not the product of Mary and *some other guy*? No, because even if it is God, whose identity was held to be male, the shame is unavoidable: Joseph is a cuckold.

So we have one parent, Mary, who venerates and serves and bows before the identity of her son, protects him and defends him against all comers and who is in the end rejected by

Jesus, who tells her to go away, that he has no family. In the end, Jesus (like those awful "kids of today") has very little to do with his parents and actually sends his mother away from him. The kid was better, higher, smarter and diviner than his parents or for that matter than any of his elders from the time of 12 years on. Don't all kids believe they are? Is this good modeling, or simply a psychologically accurate mirror of what often happens between kids and their parents?

The other "parent," Joseph, is hurt, sullen and grouchy from the beginning and ends up being quite irrelevant to Jesus or Mary or anyone else. About all we know is that he helped protect the infant Jesus at the birth, that he was a carpenter and that he felt betrayed. Now how do we see these models in the Holy Family for the "traditional family"? One answer is that they are certainly not the rosy cheerful family that Pathological Christianity seems to be promoting in its buffed up imagery. There is too much hurt, suffering, misunderstanding, animosity and general realness for that impeccable fantasy about family. What we see represented in the Holy Family is something of the Ordinary Family of today. There are misinterpretations and rifts between parents; the boy is overprotected, feminized and too highly esteemed by his mother and spends far too little time with his estranged father. We hear from thinkers in men's psychology that many men are over-feminized and fathers estranged, and that this is the result of post-industrial society. Apparently the process is prototypically considerably older.

But so what? Jesus still finds his destiny. He does what he must, what he knows deep inside is right for him and believes is right for others. Perhaps the focus on family and on the influence of family or on guarding or attending to gender roles and "civil rights" is a little misguided or at least forever being misunderstood. Perhaps there is no such thing as family or societal or world destiny, only the destiny and meaning of the individual; or even that what the individual does is indeed the meaning of family or societal or world destiny. What is clear is that no simple interpretation of the deeply psychological and symbolic relations of the members of the Holy Family can tell us all there is to know.

e) guidance given to adolescents through those painful years of moving into adulthood

Perhaps the most awkward and outlandish period of life is that transition interval between childhood and adulthood, a period of ill-defined and idiosyncratic duration in which we move from the innumerable pains, enchantments and frustrations of childhood to the suffering, fulfillments and desolations of adulthood. It seems as if all the good and ill of both adulthood and childhood condense and deluge the hapless adolescent, producing that characteristic egotism, temporary psychosis and amazement that all parents except the most inanimate and stupid recognize with both delight and repulsion. No culture has really known how to cope effectively with this transition time. Despite the fanciful and ingenuous imagery forwarded by utopians and whiners over the lost tribal past, every culture has been stymied about adolescents, accepting persons in two categories, adult and child. Numerous, imaginative rituals have been honed in worldwide cultures for celebrating puberty and the arrival of adulthood, but their purpose has been to boost the kid into adulthood as soon as possible, not to investigate or comprehend or dwell on the transition points. American society did not create adolescence but has encouraged and glorified an adolescent style of thought, feeling and behavior--without giving any helpful message to adolescents about how to cope with and manage the fears, frustrations, confusions and misinformation that comes with being a teenager.

As an adolescent, I was forever in deep straits in school or church, because I refused to be quiet about questions that stimulated my curiosity. I wanted to probe deeper, always, than my teachers were willing to go. As we studied Jesus, I wanted to fathom his model in the dark practicalities of life. I wanted to know what he **did** or would do in similar situations as I encountered. I was little interested in that anile, passive and tame form of activity referred to as "prayer and faith." The attitude appeared totally unworthy of Christ, whom I saw as active, animated, challenging, dissatisfied with the obedient and mindless life. I imagined a Jesus who would laugh and consider forthrightly an adolescent male who asked him if he masturbated, why he never apparently dated girls, what his view was about being such a mommy's boy, how he felt about having a grouchy and pouty father, why he didn't have kids, what he did in his spare time or with incredible boredom--all the questions that might be of interest to any adolescent. I thought Jesus was a lot tougher than to be offended by whether someone got (or talked about) erections but my terrified and anguished Sunday School teacher quite evidently did not think Jesus should be subjected to such inquiry.

Answers were apparently forthcoming neither from Jesus in person nor any churchy folks I met, who were unanimously appalled and aghast at my heretical carnal concerns. Because I respected Jesus and carried little admiration in my heart for those hypocritical pansies who were masquerading as teachers, ministers and the like. I sought, alas, in vain for direct guidance in the life of Jesus.

I found exactly nothing of direct use or guidance to me in the particular aches of adolescence, sex and boredom. That aberration called by evangels the "youth minister" valiantly sought to make things *interesting* to us kids while plugging the party line of prayer, abstinence and purity, but none of that washed, since it was so utterly incongruent with human experience, and told me nothing of what Jesus actually experienced while he was--church phrase--"fully human." In addition, the "youth minister" seemed to have a particular predilection for newly ripened girls, as I found out from a knockout fourteen year old named, to my dismay, "Cherry."

So there it stands.   One quite important measure of humanity and mature adulthood is the negotiation of adolescence and the acceptance and integration of the burdens and raptures of adulthood through love, work and play.   What does Jesus teach us about all this through his story? Very little of direct use to us.   Pathological Christianity makes endless proclamations about "Christian living," but neglects to inform us that these precepts have almost nothing to do with the story of Christ and almost everything to do with the idiosyncratic teachings and private obsessions of Paul.

Jesus never peregrinated the potholed, perplexing and remarkable road of living in sexual and emotional intimacy with a woman, nor had he raised children; nor did he live to middle age with its ordeals. He barely makes it into his thirties. As he hangs out with the fellows, he is continuously speaking in the mode of fables and indirections. He is obsessed with death and his destiny and thus was distinct from his chums--called his disciples.   He apparently had no friends, but was above or beyond the mere practice of individual intimacy: is that being "fully human"?

Please understand that I see these would be fine, good and extraordinary mysteries if they were ever addressed reasonably and intelligently, without the guile of condemnation. Can not a divine being like Jesus withstand hearty scrutiny? Apparently not, since such questions are answered by rhetoric of the ilk of "be still and know that only God knows the answers to such questions, whose answers you will find out if you are among the Chosen in Heaven."

And certainly the Divine Master does show us countless answers for at least the stilling of the anxious heart in the midst of unnerving conditions. To claim that answers to the dreary and often ominous and valuable questions of life on earth are answered somehow in the corpus of speculation called Christianity or even more ludicrously in some very narrow-minded, recent and careless American version of it is an outrage, impossibly stupid. There simply are not answers to all of life's problems in the story of Christ. The primary problem solved is the model of how to die. Jesus did not show us how to raise a family, but he did show us how to die well.

The Holy Family shows us in their story that there always was and always will be complexity and mystery in what we call "family." We do not see what recent evangels call "the traditional family," but a family that is living through confusions, shifting allegiances, emotional tensions and adversity, familiar to some degree in every family. It is for this reason that they are the Holy Family or the prototypical model of family, not because they demonstrate some ideal of perfection in relationships with each other. The Holy Family shows us that even a family in duress can be a place of divinity and transcendence. They proclaim by their story that a rigid and adamant version of family is unnecessary and that by the very strangeness and challenge the Holy Family embodies, there is that unique strength that leads to something interesting and new.

What is Pathological about Pathological Christianity in its view of family is the refusal to see how weird, impossible, absurd and therefore brilliant the story of the Holy Family is. When the evangel claims that we are part of the family of Christ, how little he seems to recognize that this means that literally "anything goes," rather than meaning that the way is straight and narrow. He refuses to see the oddness of the imagery.

For example, let's look at the parentage of Jesus. Christianity claims to be monotheistic, that is to have a single God with three aspects--God Father, Son and Holy Spirit--that are all one. What this means is that in some strange way, Jesus (being part of the one single God) is his own father and impregnated Mary. What this means about his relationship with his mother boggles the mind. It also seems a little humorous when we think of some of our gutter slang about men and their mothers. It is not a matter of disrespect or merely provocation to think or speak of such things. It just doesn't do to keep still and have faith about such things when stories such as that of the Holy Family have had such profound effect on billions of people while keeping them in benighted unconsciousness about their implications for us. When the psychological understanding of the events related in a sacred book can help us enrich our understanding of self and other and history and ultimate meanings, no questions should be diverted or ignored, but brought as cleanly and directly into the light as we can possibly bring them.

A Note on Abortion and *The Christian Army*

The reason fundamentalist Christians are against abortion is only partly to do with the bandied about view of the "sanctity of life" and everything to do with *making armies of Christian Soldiers*. All fundamentalist movements have been against birth control of any kind for their members, because to limit the number of children born limits the number of recruits to the force. A low birth rate limits the number of soldiers "on our side" in the dangerous future. It could happen, *God forbid,* that the "others" outnumber us some day. So, let's make babies, make a good plan of attack, get them "in" young and gather the mass force to totally dominate. Go team (God willing)!

Now how can we demonstrate that this is correct? Well the evangelists are only protesting abortion in the U.S., where as everyone knows, the only real Christians live. You don't see American evangelists going to China or Taiwan to protest abortion there. They are only protecting America, England, Ireland and other heavy-duty Christian countries. They are "us."

Chapter 6. *A Christian Psychology*

A TRUE CHRISTIAN PSYCHOLOGY would be interested in how the unconscious of the individual Christian reflects all the characters, dynamisms and archetypes of those parts of the story of Christ. In a Christian psychology that is faithful to the Bible, the Christian must find himself working to discover what aspect of his or her character not only reflects Jesus, but also Pontius Pilate, Lazarus, Mary Magdalen, the disciples, the apostles, Paul, God the Father, God the Holy Spirit, all of those figures and representations and people and manifestations of deity in the story of Christ.

A Christian psychology is not only about Christ, because Christ does not exist in a vacuum, and has no meaning nor form except in the context of the story. The *entire* story is the story of Christ, all characters are part of him and his story. His words, the words that others say about him, the stories, the fables, the teachings, the reactions, even the soldiers who crucify him are part of the story, thus part of each Christian.

The Jesus we imagine is not in a business suit or shopping in a mall, but is the Christ of his time. Any vision of Christianity means visions of the time and geography of a Palestinian desert, Jesus walking by the sea surrounded by completely arid lands, with followers who have never seen microwaves or televisions. They are people living without modern conveniences, but not without the same anxieties or confusions we have today.

One of the absurdities of Christianity in our day is that to be a Jesus one must seem to be a first-century Israelite, carrying the thoughts and responses of a middle easterner in an arid, dangerous country, an impossibly absurd and therefore delightful task. To be a Christian, if one were to respect the psychology, would mean to really find all those human and divine stories in our psyches.

You can go into any general interest book store today and find several volumes dedicated to understanding individual psychology through the analogies and imagery of Greek and Roman "myths." It is commonly understood today in popular psychology (though rejected as an approach by many true scholars of mythology) that the gods and heroes of Greek or other myths are instructive as basic or archetypal stories of individual psychology and can give us some guidance and understanding of our personal psychology.

Numerous writers have used the gods, goddesses and heroes as reflections or models of character, a practice which was popular in the Renaissance as well. Thus we have the concept in this approach of the "Apollo" type of man or "Athena" style of woman, with extensive descriptions of what the characteristics of these "types" are. The Twentieth Century has been obsessed with the practice of typology and categorization of humans into discrete, understandable, bite-sized chunks, perhaps a response to the amount of chaos, upheaval and disorder we've known these last one hundred years.

Such use of mythological characters can often illuminate particular unconscious roles or influences on how individuals see themselves and respond to other people. I won't attempt to give any detail or describe the particular attributes of these mythic figures, though I'll give a model of a "Christian" version which I think might actually be more useful and closer to our psychology than these rather remote myths.

We know that looking at stories of deities or culture heroes and their actions in all kinds of situations described in the myths has for many people from the earliest times helped them deepen the view they have of their own actions, helped them feel less alone, since themes of suffering, betrayal, loss, salvation or freedom can be shown to have been shared by all people at all times. Hearing the stories of other people has a healing power in itself, quite outside of any interpretations or explanations of the meaning of the psychology which permeates any story.   The gods and goddesses and tricksters and heroes which speak, think and act in these stories enrich our view of the world, and help us see our own little lives as part of a great, magnificent drama being played out in the warp and weave of time.

One problem with the whole enterprise of using myths is that most modern (at least American) people have not had a "classical education" in which emphasis was put on Greek and Latin literature. Most of us were not brought up in the way that European schoolchildren were until recently, reading profusely, memorizing and reciting passages from Classical Literature in their original languages. Thus many of us today have little direct personal   experience,   reactions   or   associations   with   the characters in these stories. They are a little abstract and remote. We no longer have the base for the kinds of allusions to classical imagery that were daily fare among educated people in earlier times. How many people know the source or meaning to such images as "the thread of Ariadne," "the sword of Damocles," or "to sow dragon's teeth"?

In a typical twist of irony, however, it must be mentioned that the classical heroes, gods and goddesses are being reborn in television and print comics and cartoons, though merely their names are being used to give substance to the character of some modern "superhero" or another. Some kids do as a result know today much more than their parents. Another source of "mythic stories" in kids' lives is the game Dungeons and Dragons, but this is an aberrant kind of amnesia about the actual old stories, since the characters bear more similarity to the writings of

Tolkein and recent modern fantasy writers than to the actual mythic tales.

In many senses the whole recent "psychological interest" in classical heroes and the like is a fabrication. Many people who have never read a syllable of Classical literature, but who have read Jean Bolen's books or seen the *Power of Myth* programs with Joseph Campbell or books about "the hero" or "archetypes within," use the names of gods and heroes freely. In these "interpretive books" the authors retell the stories in their own words, summarizing them and making particular "guiding" comments about them as they go alone, extracting the "lesson" from their reading (or perhaps even *reading of someone else's reading*). The reader has only the "canned" version of the story, which is modified or chosen from what are often many, many versions of the same story, a kind of shaved down, dim, dry, "instructive" version of a story which in its original was a thing of liveliness, a gripping good tale. These authors have dimmed and dulled the lights of the story with their "synopses" and turned them into sources of "sermonettes." Their versions of the myths are about as exciting as hearing the preacher give a sermon about "Revitalizing Your Marriage."

When I was a budding Jungian psychologist, I read all these Swiss and German and British authors, with all their stupendous and broad knowledge of Classical Literature. They could speak in detail and out of a lifetime of reading, conversation and study in a culture which valued classic literature about Hermes, Herakles, Heraclitus and Herodotus, Apollo and Athena. I felt I had been cheated by not being forced to recite the Aenid in memorized Latin or any of the other gruesome tortures that were commonplace in the schooling of children a century ago in Europe.

I sweated bullets trying to memorize the names, attributes and symbols of each and every one of the gods and goddesses, tricksters, folk heroes and the like. No matter how hard I tried, it would not quite "catch," partly because I knew no one at all in my daily life who was conversant in these allusions, or even cared. Such thinking is lost to us, and unless it were to be standard again in our schools (it will not), I am afraid that despite the heroic measures of many imaginal psychologists and writers, nothing of the sort will ever take a deep root in us as a culture-wide phenomenon again.

The stories that did influence me, and that continue to influence us in the West, whether we are "professing Christians" or not, are those of the Bible. It is these Judeo-Christian stories that are the archetypal images of what we are today, more than the images of Greeks and Romans (although clearly there is overlap in themes and imagery, as there is among all the world's stories). The "Christian" or the "Jewish" story are the stories that inform us of what we think feel and know. They are the closest prototypes for our behavior, actions and the value we assign to those actions.

I remember sitting for hours and hours in the winter, looking at pictures in my grandmother's richly illustrated German Bible. I couldn't read German, but it didn't matter, since I already knew the stories in English. The stories of the Bible are far less remote from our culture. especially with the renewed interest kindled by fervent evangels (although recent research has shown that far fewer people have read or know the stories of the Bible than in 1900). The stories are much more widely known and taught than the tale of King Minos or the deeds of Perseus.

The pictures and the evocation these illustrations in the German Bible made in my imagination were what mattered, not the conceptual and righteous sermons and threats that the preacher made about these stories and pictures on Sunday morning. His moralizing and the condemnations and the fire and brimstone had nothing whatsoever to do in my experience with the rich, enticing, dramatic images that I saw when I read the stories and looked at those pictures. His ranting and raving had to do with his own fears and need to impress the congregation with his interpretation; his righteousness, his moral uprightness and all of that had nothing whatsoever to do with Jesus walking on the water or putting mud on the eyes of the blind man to heal his vision.

It makes sense to make a Christian psychology based on the stories of the Bible, not based on "their lessons", but rather on a deep psychological understanding of the drama of the soul as represented in the characters of Bible. If they are truly characters that speak to soul, and not merely cardboard images, they should be able to speak directly to us and through us, since they live not so much in history as in the unconscious of humans.

A Christian depth psychology is not one based on so-called "Biblical principles," or on idealizations or ideas. It isn't based on a message of salvation nor on some historical Jesus or Solomon or Mary Magdalene. It is based on the way the story of Christ, his family, friends and enemies and doubters and the faithful.

A Christian *psychotherapy* worthy of the name focuses on the rich and varied imagery of Christian lore, history and thinking. It would be an experience of richness and psychological power rather than one of dead abstractions, moralizing, lifeless political admonitions and crazy formulas about "salvation." It would begin to see through Christianity rather than seeing only the surface of Christianity or the "concept" of Christ. It would be an invitation to abundance in soul, in thinking and feeling rather than to psychological poverty, deprivation, guilt and stupid narrowness so drilled in by Pathological Christianity.

Heaven and Hell, Apocalypses, Raptures, Salvation--all those once stirring images which have deteriorated into empty walls would be opened to psychological imagination of the kind that Dante and Blake once used to enrich and deepen our soul into the worlds of existence that Christ spoke of when he said, The Kingdom of Heaven is within you.

Christianity is always trying to promote itself as the "universal religion," open to anyone. Christ is portrayed as holding his arms open for all to come. The only way, however, that we could all come to Christianity is for it to truly open its arms, and its psychology, to all. This means throwing away all moralizing, all politicizing, all attempts to prescribe how the world should be and replacing such action with the perspective of a psychology. This means neither eliminating political action itself, nor working for better housing or better conditions for the poor, jobs, or finer education. It merely means dropping the "prescriptions" for other people's behavior, whether *they* should do one thing or another, and dropping collective action, mass hysteria and collective tyranny, and taking one's personal responsibility to change the world through *respect for all things and ways, and irreverence for all things and all ways.*

Christ made it abundantly clear that he was utterly uninterested in rules, politics or money but rather in *saving his own soul by doing and being exactly what he was,* by cleaning up his own soul. Again, Jesus did not exist in a vacuum. He was surrounded by the rich world of political turmoil, religious variety, wealthy and poor, disease, joy and suffering. He merely lived and taught as he could. He'd very possibly have been another forgotten or barely remembered Apocalyptisist or religious prophet if it hadn't been for Paul, who promulgated stories of the life and what he began to promote as the "lessons" of Christ throughout the land. Paul was a terrific P.R. man, tireless, masochistic, convinced, and very intense. His self-hatred, hatred of his own body, guilt, zealousy and ambitions are clearly the model for Pathological Christianity with its load of abomination of the natural passions and desires of the living, breathing world. Christ, looking at what Paul and his ilk have done to what he said and done, might exclaim, "*Thank God I am Christ and not a Christian!*"

A Christian Depth Psychology would not exclude anyone because he or she is not of the same *religion*. It recognizes that "religion" is entirely determined by social and economic pressures rather than by some profound meaning at the heart of things. A Christian Depth Psychology is not a religious perspective at all but a perspective which trusts that there is something truly universal in Jesus's story, not just something that those who act or walk or look a certain way are involved in. This would take seriously that Jesus is a *Christ*, with the true importance that Christians would say he has, rather than a petty formal, ritualistic, history-bound, behavior-bound, event-bound credo which excludes people who do not blindly accept the message and deeply pathologizes those who do accept.

A widened and deepened view of Jesus as a particular embodiment of *Christ* differentiates the work of depth psychotherapy from that of *Christian Counseling*, which is merely political indoctrination. The impact of this kind of Christian psychology would be an invitation for people who are profoundly repulsed by the narrowing and silting in of the once great channel of Christ. It would automatically include those who see value in the story of Christ, no matter what their interpretation or understanding or belief or conclusions about the Christ story happens to be. This psychology, like all depth psychology, is an attitude more than a science, religion or political position. It is a view of inclusion, of treating one's own Holy Cow and everybody else's Holy Cow with the same respect and the same irreverence.

It is time for us to recognize, with humor and delight, rather than with fear or loss, that all religion, science, all human endeavors are activities of the psyche, both serious and absurd.

A Christian Psychology worthy of the name values the soul and its splendid imagination and creativity. It takes the stories of the Bible seriously as stories, as extraordinary speech about life, products of the psyche as valuable, though not more valuable than dreams, folktales or daydreams or Science. It also recognizes that the Bible has a particular place of interest and must have touched a root of unconscious to have been treasured and respected in so many people's homes. A Christian Psychology takes this to heart and sees the archetypal place of honor of the Bible and Bible stories. It sees all this as a deep stirring of soul, so profound that it can't possibly be the subject of evangelism or "edifying sermons" by people with "ministries" who can't see the infinite importance of these stories but instead whine and carp and whinny about little passing fads in human existence such as what candidate to vote for or what television show is all right to watch.

A Christian depth psychotherapy will take all the characters of the Christ story as part of the story of the human soul. Thus the soul of each person carries the seed of Christ, Lazarus, Peter, Pontius Pilate, Mary Mother of Jesus, the woman at the well and all other characters in this sage story of the human unconscious. Each of us carries the Savior and the Saved, and the story of longing, suffering and rebirth is within each psyche. This is what the Christ story gives us, not some set of precepts or rules.

The process of a depth psychotherapy which has at its heart the Christ story will be attentive to dreams, feelings, thoughts, family patterns and relationships which re-enact some facet of the Christ story. A mid-life crisis might, for example, be something like when a disciple of Jesus lays down his ordinary work and daily life in order to follow some profound calling to "higher work." When Jesus confronted the woman at the well about her adultery, this reminds us of the call to consciousness that can come when any of us awakes from a trance about what we are doing in our lives--in current terms--Jesus confronted her "denial." The many parables that Jesus told, such as the story of the Prodigal Son, are far more valuable as stories of the human soul (in this case, forgiveness of one's self for making a youthful error of judgment which can be forgiven by our more mature self) than they are practical lessons in how to live our daily life. Jesus on the cross is more a striking and profound parallel of sacrificing one's self for an eloquent and critical meaning in one's life than it is a story about a single deity washing clean all transgression for the entirety of all future and past populations. What profound meaning in the individual human soul does this event have? Such a question will bear far more fruit than some abstract, preachy missionizing of people to Pathological Christianity for ulterior political goals.

The Adoration of the Christ Child, the precociousness of Jesus in the temple, his going on his teaching sojourn, the invitation for whores, tax collectors, misfits and crooks into his company, the changing of water to wine at the marriage feast in Canaa, the raising Lazarus from the dead, the entreating of the disciples to stay awake with him the night before his crucifixion, the joys, doubts, wonderment and transfiguration of the disciples, the appearance of Jesus after death to Mary and to Thomas--all such stories are parallels to the experience of the human soul as it peregrinates the time from birth to death and perhaps beyond. Pathological Christianity misses the depth, universality and strength of such images, metaphors and direct speech to the soul that these stories give by focusing on them as *literalisms*. The Christ story is far deeper than some historical or metaphysical nonsense about *what we must do* or *how we must act* or *what will happen at the end of time.*

Of course, many Christians will find the idea of seeing the Christ story as a story of psyche as blasphemous and sacrilegious, because they are trained to see the story as literal and concrete, like some sort of Lesson Book. It is just fine if we wish to see Apollo or Odysseus as symbolic of a heroic urge in ourselves, but these personages, being remote from our beliefs can be seen as "merely fantasy characters." They can be taken as metaphors. When someone dares suggest that Jesus is less a figure of historical importance than as a symbolic (however important and profound) representation of the individual soul finding its way through the world, Pathological Christians act as if something were being taken away from Christ's significance. Jesus reminds us in his own life of the likeliness and isolation that a person feels when he tries to bring something into consciousness that people do not want to hear. His is the story of the unconscious becoming conscious, and the hell that breaks loose when that happens. It is not the story of acquiescence and mindless acceptance of anything, but rather, provocation, dispute and anarchy from the established norms. Christ's story is about the individual soul against the collective and the refusal to accept what is demanded by the Pharisees--the comfortable, conservative corporation of his time or our time.

Pathological Christianity demands that each word, each syllable, each event, each saying, every single incident in the Bible, from the Creation story to the Apocalypses vision in Revelations, is a literal, historical fact sheet, directly transcribed in methodical historical precision. It demands a grim, humorless reverence toward the Bible, and refuses to see it as the thing that all religious stories are--which is a *psychology of the human soul*, a metaphor and prototype of what each individual souls traverses in its development. The Bible, like all sacred and holy texts, is a book of symbolic psychology.

Christians like to see the story of Christ as universal. To see the Christ story as symbolic psychology, to inform a psychotherapy with this story, is a recognition of the eternal existence of Christ as manifested in many Christs of many cultures and many ages. The story need not be localized and specified to Jesus only (which deadens and closes it off to all but a few people), but seen as an unending and forever deepening story of human experience.

Or is it that it is frightening to look at the Jesus story and what it tells us about our character and we cannot risk being frightened?

If we played out the story of Jesus, we would see that we completely lack information about his teenage or young adult years, so it is very difficult for us to know what makes up a Christ at these ages. We know a great deal about Buddha's adolescence and young adulthood, but so very little about that of Jesus. It is as if the Christian story chooses to ignore these difficult ages as being too problematical for the story. The experience of old age also is difficult to understand in the light of Jesus' example since he didn't live to advanced years..

It appears that as far as the story of JC goes, to be "Christ-like," we have to be a highly prized and worshipped boy, a know-it-all smart aleck twelve year old and a very intense, very alone, otherworldly, strange, antisocial male in young middle age. If we go on the model of Jesus alone, this is about all the guidance we get through his model, and it is, as any child will tell you, the way and not the words that make the influence.

If you describe the acts and events of Christ, what he did, how he was, line by line as a story to a parent of a teenager and asked if this is how they would like their kid to act, would there be one in a thousand who would say yes?

Psychology and Religion

Psychology, and in psychotherapy in particular, is a child of religion and religious practices. For psychology or any social science to claim the hard sciences as parent is a little like a sunflower claiming that a trout is his father. They may be related in some cosmic way, but in the simple and direct way we understand things, they are just not part of the same immediate family.

If anything, the so-called hard sciences (chemistry, physics, etc.) are the children of psychology, of a particular way of thinking, feeling and behaving. Academic psychologists sometimes want to demonstrate that a psychological researcher uses what is called scientific method in his research. This is apparently in the hope that the reputation of psychology will be "elevated" into being a "science." Thus we see the psychology of science and its grip on our definition of the "real." The assumptions of science, however, are just as fantastical and unprovable as those of Pathological Christianity. Actually, the basic expectation of both is the same: that what they demonstrate each in their own method will be recognized, accepted and praised by anyone who sees it.

Psychology ought to know better than science, since it is vastly older. As a matter of fact, psychology is, or should be, religion grown older and wiser. As long as psychology is hoodwinked by the old devil trick of *certainty*, through theories or the influence of Pathological Christianity, it will always be juvenile and territorial, and never wise, amused and astute.

Because psychology has ignored or forgotten its lineage in religion it has split itself off from its own main tasks, helping people to find meaning in life and prepare for death. It's been said much but bears repeating that the word psychotherapy means "care of psyche," not just stopping smoking or "learning how to express anger" or "getting in touch with my inner child" or reducing anxiety through hypnosis. These things fall away immediately when a deeper sense of meaning is found, and that is what Pathological Christianity knows and purports to give, but never can give, since it is tied too much with money, power, politics and collective control.

Popular psychology and advertising in America focus on many social concerns and health-related questions such as smoking, diet and weight control. Consider the problem of weight control and its relationship with life-changing psychotherapy. We know that a real weight reduction plan cannot be only diet and exercise, since these activities focus on the body exclusively. Even what is called "mind control" in these programs is still just body discipline. Such approaches don't feed what is so hungry in the human person (the Self), but rather what is not hungry (the body). The real hunger in humans is to feel good, secure, happy and satisfied.

If a fat person feeds a psyche (Greek: *butterfly*) what it wants to eat, the soul will become interested in food rather than merely consuming it.   Food becomes something intriguing, something to enjoy rather than something to merely stuff down. Psyche feeds on images.   When we attend with simple enjoyment to dreams, to aesthetic pleasure, to natural beauty, to our thoughts and feelings, when we walk and read and think and work in the garden or observe nature, we develop flexibility and move around--we don't just sit and eat.   Our bodies move and it is impossible to be truly fat.   One simply wants to move and explore and enjoy the world.   Fat is immovability.   I saw an article about a woman who weighed 1,189 pounds and the thing that impressed me the most was that she was so fat she *could not move*.

Tending to all these things in the psyche (not rigidly but with regularity) will result in a natural movement toward balance in the body because they arise from natural desires for health and action--the natural desire for *work*.   There is no greater waste in America than our view and practice of retirement, and you can see the dark effects of this on the majority of men over 65. Retirement is not inaction, but time to make meaning in life and prepare for death.   Would it not be interesting if every Social Security recipient was required to have good psychotherapy or work on their soul as part of the requisite for payment?

When psychology severed its friendship and marriage with religion it alienated people and ended by making itself ugly, stupid and inaccessible to most everyone, especially to many Christians or other spiritual seekers.   Without the healing balance of a natural psychology, religious doctrinizers such as the evangelist invent personal and private psychologies based on their own personal suffering, idiosyncrasies, pain, pleasure and politics.

By not addressing the natural interest in death and ultimate meaning that religions attend to, much of psychology

has become a dry, impotent husk. It has ended by taking on all
sorts of macabre and silly New Age masks or masks from other
tribal traditions which, shoplifted from their context in Stone
Age cultures, are pure idiocy and farce.

A reflective person who has treated himself to self-
analysis and a natural way of life is a threat to both psychology
and religion today. A reflective person thinks, feels and behaves
in ways congruent with values which arise out of a deep
confrontation with his own soul and not with the advertisements
and allurements of Professional Religion whether in the direct
guise of Pathological Christianity or "psychotherapy." He has
worked to integrate the dark and light forces in his being, and
not taken things for granted. Such a confrontation of self
certainly does not exclude a Christian orientation as part of its
result, but it does not automatically include any belief or thought
either. What it does demand is a kind of raw honesty and a
willingness to live in ambiguity, sometimes terrifying ambiguity,
which the individual knows will inevitably lead to some
uncertainty about things in life for which it might be very
soothing to pretend certainty. Confronting your delusions and
the delusions of your culture demands courage.

Chapter 7. *Sex and Pathological Christian Conditioning*

THERE IS NO PLACE FOR HUMAN SEXUALITY within Pathological Christianity. Better said, there is no place for sexual excitement and joy. It is true there are mountains of books written about sexuality from a "Christian perspective." They are without fail, however, either political doctrines or joyless abstractions about sexuality as a "gift of God," "a deep sacrament," the "fulfillment of marriage," or the "wonder of procreation." Never for pure animal pleasure or *fun.*

Nowhere is the body actually to be found in any of these pronouncements, but rather some ghostly clean-scrubbed spirits cheerfully engaging in disembodied and sanitary acts for the "glory of God," and the "sanctity of marriage."

Attention to the joys of juices, heat, erections, frictions, ejaculations, grimaces, releases, thrusts, pain and pleasure, loss of control, howling, screaming or ecstasy are not just given little attention in texts about "Christian sexuality"--they are utterly ignored. It's *not nice* to talk about such things, so their consideration is out of the question. It is not just a question of *sexual matters* being dirty, rude and nasty, but all "raw pleasures", all basic physical sensualities and deep bodily pleasures.

It is as if the act of "getting saved" suddenly sucks all the juices and hot fantasy, all the grinding erotic dynamism right out of people. It converts the skin to Herculon or Teflon, as if Christ were some Stain Master who coated each body in such a way that no dirt, sweat, blood or semen could penetrate, but rather be wiped off, swished in the sink where with a flick of the switch it is driven into some dark sewer. If it all clogs up, we call Jesus Christ--Roto-Rooter Man--to untangle and pull the coagulations free from the stinking pipes. Presto! clean again!

Most of us know too well, sooner or later even the most efficient pipe can get clogged and backed up. Christian women want to hide their menstrual bleeding from the awareness of others. This bleeding is a mark which demonstrates that unlike men, women are really *not quite saved.* They are too tempted to be aware of the juices and functions of the body. We must keep our dirty bodies covered and scrubbed. Remember that a speck of dusty already starts the downhill rush toward filthiness.

Women are always suspect in this whole matter of sexuality. They are the pipe-cloggers and the source of awareness of our sinful corpulence since they are more likely to be reminded of their body at least once a month, and not just of the body in general, but of the genitals!

Men can pretty much forget about their bodies, and most do, for long periods of no periods, but women seem to always *have something going on down there.*

"What's the matter with mom?" Thanks to television, the real sex *educator* of our day, everybody knows but no one is saying, because to say reminds us of the body.

It is common knowledge that women's personalities change, or actually, their true personalities come out when they are "on the rag." In other words, the menses, that event that reminds women of their true, sex mad, demonic character, brings out their witchiness, their clinginess, their aberrant grouchiness.

The body reminds us of our nature and our animal origin. Thinking about any of this leads to nothing but sin, sin, sin.

Talk about sin and sex brings us right to the heart of the beast, that is, fornication and adultery. This means any act of raw excitement, to the evangelical, but gets concentrated in the notion of sex outside of the holy bonds of matrimony.

Sex before or outside of marriage is sinful in precisely the same way that dessert before dinner is wrong. In other words, you shouldn't have what you crave until you are too full to enjoy it. The rules are a little different depending on whether you are a man or a woman, however.

Because they don't have menses and are therefore unconscious of the body, Christian men can get away with affairs. A Christian man has an affair unconsciously and out of the seduction of woman, so it's a pardonable thing. A woman who has an affair is a double sinner, because she was aware of her genitals all the while, thus is eternally guilty of premeditation.

Christian men can be forgiven, but Christian women cannot.

Pathological Christians are sex-crazed and sex-mad in ways that those without the bug cannot be because they are obsessed. In order to avoid the seduction of sexual sin, one must be aware of and the potential for sex all the time. This is especially true for women whose notorious neediness, loneliness, and weakness (especially around menses time) and *self-touching* make them specially prey to sex madness.

Jeanette told me that because of her training to be always on the lookout for sin, especially sexual sin, she was always and continuously afraid she would be sexual or have sexual feelings unexpectedly. If she would accidentally brush up against someone on the school bus, for example, she was terrified her breasts might touch the other person and she might experience a sexual thought or feeling--commit a sin. Even though it might be a pure accident, she'd still be to blame (she reasoned) if she felt pleasure. After she began to date, she reviewed every single action or thought about the boy to discover whether she had, in fact, committed a sin.

She couldn't wash herself in the bathtub without being worried that she'd transgressed.

Rather than developing into a person who was led away "from the temptation of sin," into "higher things," Jeanette had sex continually on her mind. Despite constant praying, church attendance, Bible reading and study, she became sexually focused, constantly ruminating, fantasizing and thinking about sexual sin.

Is Jeanette's story unusual among evangelical Christians? Not at all. Certainly many people are able to suppress thoughts about sex or sin more effectively than Jeanette, and claim that the rigid effects of pathological Christianity do not drive them to obsess about sex, but the denial of these effects simply produces symptoms in other areas: weight gain or anorexia, depression, manic episodes or addictions or just plain meanness. We cannot all channel our sexual drives into helping the poor like saints, though many Christians have attempted to drive down the devil of sexual passion by the accumulation of wealth, power and influence.

More likely, surreptitious sex is performed in secret and self-hatred by these Christians, who try to maintain a halo of purity and virginity on the outside

It is impossible to overestimate the range or depth of damage done by this hypocrisy. The attempt to portray the "righteous, sinless life" rather than directly integrating a realistic, tolerant and effective communication about sex has taken staggering tolls on us psychologically, medically, financially, politically, intellectually, in every way imaginable. Pathological Christian insistence on unconsciousness about sex is responsible for sexually transmitted diseases, child molestation and every other perversion. Rather than curing pornography, evangelical Christianity is the impetus for its existence, for without the unnatural inhibitions about human sexuality, there would be no need for the huge industry serving the powerful desires behind those inhibitions.

Pornography is clearly the invention of fundamentalisms such as evangelical Christianity, because it confuses love and power. Pornography is political, not sexual. It is about control, domination and submission of the weak to the powerful. Since Christianity claims that the majority of sexual acts engaged in by people are acts of evil, instead of perfectly natural and normal acts engaged in by humans since the beginning of our existence, sex becomes an arena of will power and domination rather than an act of intimate connection between human beings.

Randy Forton is a Methodist minister. He and his wife of 25 years, Laura, have two sons, who are grown . One of the sons is married with two young children. The other, Paul, recently confessed to his parents with great fear about their judgment that he is gay and living with his lover in a small town in Missouri.

Two years ago Randy and Laura would immediately have expressed shock and dismay toward Paul, and insisted that he speak with a Christian counselor, read the Bible, and ask Jesus to help him mend his ways.

However, things have gotten very complicated for Randy and Laura themselves recently, since Randy now has AIDS, and has been forced to reveal to Laura that he has had homosexual affairs all his married life and before their marriage as well.

Laura had no idea that Randy was bisexual and Randy had kept his extramarital affairs with utmost discretion, never taking chances in town with gay lovers, but making his contacts in several other places with men he trusted not to reveal their secret. He had always been considerate and attentive with Laura, responsible with money, very active in both the churches they pastored (because Laura and he always worked as a team) and generous with his time in community organizations. Randy was really a model pastor.

Then he got sick, showing at first wrenching headaches, gastrointestinal problems, weight loss and pains throughout his body, moderate at first but increasing. Randy had a strong suspicion he'd contracted HIV and consulted a doctor in another city while attending to some church business. His worst fears were sustained; and now on top of the bad news, he'd now be compelled to face Laura, the congregation and of course, God Himself, for his unfaithfulness and homosexuality.

Randy had made a kind of unconscious deal with himself that even though he preached against and sincerely believed that homosexuality was sinful against God, as long as he did good work at his church and served his family, he would "make up for the sin." Truth is, he didn't really even think about it beyond a gnawing sense that he was the "worst of sinners."

When he found he had AIDS, Randy thought first of killing himself as the best way out. He was convinced he was bound for Hell, whatever that meant, so why not just commit suicide hide the horrible facts, sparing his family, the congregation and others? However, he didn't have much of a chance to consider this option, because Laura somehow guessed that Randy had AIDS, and that it was the result of homosexual encounters. Was this a case of psychic knowledge, or simply the fact that she allowed herself to acknowledge consciously what she knew clearly in her heart all along, but couldn't bring herself to speak? Laura herself preferred the second theory.

Despite the fact that Laura was enraged, hurt, shocked and panicked by the news, she made Randy promise not to kill himself--she did know him well and understood the extent to which the necessity to cover "unsavory" information is demanded in the evangelical Christian community.

What Randy and Laura had to face was the hard reality that attempting to portray the ideals of evangelical Christianity, though apparently all to the good of the community and for the glory of God, had finally cost them their family and the community around them. These ideals, or better said, delusions and projections, had cost each of them the possibility of intimacy, directness, and the experience of authentic humanity.

Paul, the gay son, had lived for years with the terror of "being found out," of the full expectation that his parents could never understand him and would ultimately be forced by their beliefs to reject him. If Randy would not have been "found out," he admitted that he would have felt compelled to condemn his son, though he admitted that it would "tear his heart apart" to have done so.

The other son, Chad, had always sensed that "something was wrong," in his parents' relationship. He never could lay a finger on it, but he described them as "seeming hollow and fake, though they always said and did the right things." Chad had expressed a kind of "hyper-masculinity," developing into a hard-core athlete, motorcyclist and outdoorsman, while always remaining a good church-going kid. He was an Eagle Scout; he always had plenty of girlfriends, and ended up marrying a beautiful woman, Cynthia, who described him as "a real man; one of the few I've ever known who deserves the title." However, Chad confessed to being terribly afraid that he was going to be seen as weak, a sissy, especially since his brother had confided in him that he was gay, several years before.

Laura had been forced by her image of the Christian Woman to stay unconscious about what she really knew in her heart about Randy and about herself. Certainly there was evidence that Randy was not so terribly interested in her as a lover; he was frequently dysfunctional, and for several years, they had made love only once every few months. Laura was very unsatisfied sexually, but considered herself selfish and self-pitying if she thought about the topic. It wasn't just the sex, however. Her relationship with Randy had for a long time felt "wooden, formal, like a cardboard cutout of pastor and pastor's wife." However, Laura had trained herself, like many Christian women, to "be grateful before God for what I have, since it is of course God's will." After all, he provided for the family, was a respected man of God, and he didn't beat her. How dare she ask for more? Why, that would be *prideful*.

Despite their background and position, the Forton family had the strength to finally face what had come about and the reasons it had come about. Secrecy, fantasy, idealization of the goal of the "perfect family" almost had denied them the opportunity to really know and love each other, to finally be a real family with their human foibles, emotions, longings and pain.

Working with this family and with many other evangelical families who have come to the point where unavoidable humanity finally cuts through fantasy is a kind of cult deprogramming. The psychotherapist must be willing to move along with a family like this with a high degree of awareness and surgical skill, attentive to the powerful habits that the fundamentalist belief system has to pull individuals back into its power in a myriad of subtle (and not so subtle) ways.

Randy's biggest seduction, for example, was to "go up on the cross," and be crucified for all his sins, hiding behind the clever ruse of the World's Biggest Sinner. This ploy is a favorite maneuver of some Christians, a maneuver to avoid conflict with other people, and once again to be superior to others by portraying oneself as the lowest dog around. Remember that one way of getting to the front of the line in Christianity is to be the last, since Jesus said in his "Sermon on the Mount" that the first shall be last and the last first.

Of course Laura, Chad and Paul all tried to take their turns on the cross also, the whole family trying to sneak around the topics of anger, personal betrayal (versus Christian betrayal), lies and secrets in the family. Everybody wanted to take the blame once the Crucifixion Game got started.

Once that routine was blipped, another began, becoming righteous with one another. Chad wanted his father Randy to have been abstinent, to have simply "not given in to sin." Abstinence and other neat tricks, the "just say no" school of conquering sin are favorites among the cheery light-seeking angelics, who like to dream of spiritual disembodiment.

The view that abstinence (or "pray it away, give it to God" or ignoring sexual desire) is an effective way to handle the strong passions that arise in the human body and psyche is the true source of child molestation, pornography and the spread of sexual diseases. This view drives the expression of sexuality, which is as inevitable as day and night, into the dark, where we can't see what we are working with. I mean in the dark literally and psychologically: in dark secret sexual encounters between fathers and daughters, in affairs, in pornography; and psychologically, deeper into the unconscious.

People will have sex, because sex is a natural desire like eating. Just as lack of eating or fear of eating produces the dangerous and sometimes life-threatening symptoms we have come to know as the eating disorders, anorexia and bulimia, so too the terror of sex or the suppression of sexuality produce perversions or disorders of sexual expression which can ruin people psychologically, medically and financially.

Please don't tell me that we are a sexually aware culture which has somehow evolved in our treatment of sexuality, and give as evidence that people can talk openly about any sort of sexual act on television or buy any kind of magazine--or every magazine on the rack--that speaks openly and obsessively about sex. For it is the very obsessiveness with which sex is spoken about which betrays our very prudish extreme discomfort with sex and with the body.

The fact that in an age where information is readily available about the dangers of "unprotected sex" and the spread of sexually transmitted diseases (of which AIDS is only one of many), the numbers of people who get such diseases actually continues to climb shows that we are driven by unconscious rather than conscious motivation. The logical thing is to use a condom or to find out if a partner has an STD. People don't because they are still under the sway of the Christian message, which maintains that sex is sin and must stay buried and dark and not be handled, since it will bite us and send us from the Garden of Eden into Hell.

There is a fantasy which arises from the gospel of Matthew and from the Judeo-Christian tradition in general that if you think a thing it is as the same as done. The thought is the act, so it is dangerous to think. It is always dangerous to think, because you might challenge or act in ways that are not consistent with a fundamentalist precept.

This principle is the core of the problem of sin, specifically sexual sin. Until a little maturity is developed in this infantile conclusion, we will be plagued by molestation, pornography, STD's, family alienation and scores of other blocks to the rich fulfillment of our human connection with each other, and I might add, blocks to spiritual development as well.

The Forton family of which I spoke earlier actually became a family when they began to separate thought and act in this way. When they realized that they were being driven by the fear of revealing their thoughts, feelings and fantasies to each other, and began to speak the unspeakable, they found each other for the first time. It is ironic but I have found it not unusual that they each began to speak of how the freedom to speak openly actually opened up the possibility of *feeling* spiritual rather than just *acting* spiritual, as they had been doing in their Christian games.

Evangelical Christians are afraid of authentic psychotherapy (as opposed to biblical indoctrination sessions) because they are afraid that if people speak of their dark terrors or supposed aberrations without automatic biblical answers, they will automatically go astray and amuck. Nothing could be further from the truth or more opposed to what actually happens in the human psyche. What is suppressed gains power in the unconscious, whereas what is brought forth and honestly considered can be integrated into a move toward maturity.

A man who called himself "Ned" came into my office, refusing to give his real name. He lived in another city and had gotten my name from a friend of his there. He said that he had been having some "extremely disturbing thoughts" and needed to talk with someone about them, though he was afraid to reveal them to anyone in his own town. He claimed that he was well-known and respected there and that he didn't want anything to "get out" about him.

It turns out that Ned had a 15 year old daughter who was very beautiful and had developed a quite curvaceous figure. Ned had begun to fantasize about seeing her naked, and had fantasies night and day, rolling around in his head to the point where he could hardly bear to even be around his daughter "for fear of what I might do." He had thought about making a little hole in the closet next to where the girl took a shower so he could watch her. Though he had not actually done so, he was terrified he would.

Ned was an elder in his church, a Sunday school teacher for adults, and had lately been leading discussions on Paul's Letters. These texts in the later Testament contain lots of lurid judgments on fornication and the like and Ned was just sure he was getting ready to roast in his Damnation.

I shouldn't kid about this, because poor Ned was really and truly terrified in a way I have rarely seen a man of his type-- the stoic, Germanic cool kind of businessman. In a way he was right to be shaking in his skin, because he was being affected by such strong unconscious natural physical urgings. He showed me a picture of the girl and she was a knockout.

I was actually proud of this guy that he had the gumption to track down a psychologist, despite his abhorrence of psychotherapy, and to talk this thing out; not do what many men do, which is to act out some urge through pornography, prostitutes or with his daughter. He was remarkably ready for a psychological intervention and had to shed a lot of inhibition to talk to me about all of this.

Two important things were happening with this man at this moment. He was stimulated by the presence of the girl--this lively, beautiful, sexy young person who was awakening what was a kind of sleeping, unconscious young man in himself. He was frankly bored with life. He had been a go-getter in younger years, ambitious, creative and innovative in his field, and had lately just been going through the motions. He told me that young sexy women had been appearing in his dreams as well. This determined, for me, that he needed to get back to challenging himself in new ways, so I talked with him about how he could start up some new and risky adventures with his business. He didn't get the connection until I asked him if he didn't use to come home from work when he was excited and new in the field with an erection, all excited in his masculinity and ready to make love with his wife. He remembered with a smile that he had.

Speaking of this, it turned out that he and his wife had kind of gotten "disinterested" in sex, or rather, according to him, his wife had, telling him they were getting too old to be so interested in such things. It was time to outgrow them and get more interested in "spiritual things." He and his wife were only in their mid-forties.

These two factors, listlessness in his life's work and the alienation from his wife, had combined to make Ned psychologically more dead than alive. He was living *pro forma*, not really in his body or psyche at all, but a kind of cut-out of himself. So along walks his daughter (it might easily have been a young woman at work or someone he met on his business travels), and he gets this terrific rush of young energy into his well-settled and substantially petrified life, and boom! he finds himself sexually excited. All he can do is sum it up as "demonic forces" or "sin" because that is the container offered by evangelical Christianity.

He needed this jolt to restart his motor, to get him interested in life again, and that's what I told him. I said that it was perfectly natural that he'd feel sexual excitement around this young woman, even if she was his own daughter, and that the suppression of the awareness and acceptance of this event was what was making him sick inside. That, and the fact that his wife had cut him off and he'd not told her how enraged and betrayed he felt about it.

Another important element in this situation is that young people do need to be recognized and accepted as sexual beings by their parents. This is part of their growing up. This can be terribly troublesome if the parents automatically make the assumption forwarded by pathological Christianity that though equals action, because it pushes us to either toward suppress the thought as "evil" or to act out the "impulse" or thought.

It can mean so much to a girl to be recognized as beautiful and sexy by her father in a way that is safe and thoughtful. It can promote a real sense of being recognized as an attractive woman. It is a kind of sacred trust that can be invaluable to the young woman. It can be terribly destructive, however, if the father literally acts on the fantasy, is so terrified by it that he fears he'll lose control or fears that he is in the "presence of evil."

This is an example of why we need to raise up these so-called dark thoughts and work with them, bring them to discussion without fear. Attempts to reject or dismiss them gives them strength, which can lead to impulse for action if increased enough. If we develop a container, a way of talking and understanding a father's sexual attraction for his daughter as an expression of his need for renewal of his own youth and blossoming, while still prohibiting the action, yet demanding that the issue be addressed, much less molestation, pornography or violence disguising itself as sexuality will happen in our culture.

We have nothing to hide in our thoughts. It is an insult to God to think that he might punish our thoughts or fantasies; as if he could be so petty as that.

Conversely, the kinds of "talk shows" we see so frequently, or the kind of pitiful parading of fetishes and kooky images concocted by carnival shows like those given by The singer Madonna and her ilk are simply another form of hiding, another form of pathological Christianity. Madonna couldn't exist without her own Christian background and wouldn't be worth a spinning nickel if it weren't for the nervous strain of the evangelical in America. The rehearsal of so-called sexual aberrations and titillations is simply one more way to hide from talking with one another. Isn't it astonishing how often on these shows people say things that they obviously haven't said to one

another in private? This is a pretense at honesty or openness.
Intimacy is something enjoyed with the delight of privacy. It can
never be something presented as a spectacle on television.

A healthy person accepts with grace and humor a wide
spectrum of sexual expression as normal, whether he or she feels
attracted to that expression or not. A healthy person feels no
particular need to parade and exhibit his or her sexuality for
political or psychological reasons. There is never any valid
reason to hate another person or group for their preferred form
of sexual expression, nor any reason to elevate one person or
group for theirs. Only sex which is actually violence or abuse--
such as child molestation, prostitution and rape--is pathological.
It is equally pathological and violating to condemn (as
Pathological Christians do) any form of loving sexuality between
equal consenting partners as wrong, whether they be unmarried
heterosexuals or homosexuals.

PATHOLOGICAL CHRISTIANITY IS A MEN'S club
served by women. The women are given good reason to believe
their service is noble and godly and the men good reason to
believe they deserve the service.

Patrick and Jan have been married eleven years. They
have two children. In the past year, Patrick "got saved." He
began taking their family to his church on Sundays, Wednesdays
and for special events on Saturdays. Jan herself had always felt
herself to be a good practicing Christian, brought up a
Methodist, a regular church-goer, Bible reader, and "professor
of the faith." Patrick told her that her Christianity was not
"good enough," and that she'd have to come with him into his
church, which was "far more biblical, a true church of Jesus
Christ." He repudiated her upbringing, calling it "lax on real
Christian action."

Patrick has always been somewhat military in his view of
life, including childrearing, and has always found Jan too "soft"
with the kids. In his new church, the pastor had started a
program called "The Courage to Discipline," in which he
maintained that parents in the modern U.S. had been convinced
by liberals and atheists to "go soft" on their kids and that this
was the source of our big social problems in the twentieth
century. This was a good match for Patrick's own position.
Now God was on his side.

Also the pastor exhorted men in his congregation (and in
the "Christian men's groups" and "Christian Businessmen's
Breakfasts" he conducted) that it was their absolute God given
right and responsibility to take the lead to "guide and pilot" their
families. It is the standard position of leaders of "Christian
Men's" organizations that the world has gone bad in part because
men have relaxed their control on the reins of the society and the
family, letting pagans, witches, women and liberals take over. A

man's job is to take back the steering and control of the vessel, with Jesus as co-pilot.

Patrick ate this up, and attended every talk that the pastor gave at church or at men's clubs around town. He took notes during the sermons, and read the books his pastor told him to read, joined a Bible study led by the same man. Meanwhile Jan had her own responses to Patrick's growing obsession.

At first, she was glad to see Patrick interested in something, taking initiative to develop himself in some way. He'd seemed increasingly depressed for several years, isolated and dissatisfied with his job. He had stopped hunting and fishing with his friends as he once had, and appeared to have little interest in anything. Jan had essentially been raising their two kids by herself, since Patrick was so unavailable. She had even helped coach her son's soccer team, though Patrick was the one who had insisted that the boy play soccer.

Patrick appeared to come alive after his "conversion." He was more talkative, began looking more energetic and vigorous, and showed sexual interest in her for the first time in a year. He cleaned up the room he was using as a little personal "office" and made it all tidy and neat. He organized his books and a little tape recorder there. Jan was a little disconcerted that Patrick threw away a large number of books that had once been of interest to him, books on American Indians, Art and sports, and replaced them with only a few titles, several Bibles and Christian books. She just thought, however, that this was better than living with a dead person, that we all have to do some "spring cleaning" once in a while.

Soon, however, Patrick began to make increasing demands on Jan. He required her to join a women's group at the church, which she described as "a bunch of dried up cardboard people, smiling all the time and wearing cute, overly clean outfits and too much hair spray." But she did it.

He told Jan he wanted her to stop working, and stay home more with the children, since that was her "true Christian job." He also informed her that as a Christian woman she needed to work more on being "feminine." Jan had always been "outdoorsy" and had enjoyed trapshooting, camping and hunting since she was an adolescent. She went hunting as a kid with her father, and it was always a pleasure to walk in the fields, looking for birds in the cool air of fall. Patrick thought this activity was "too masculine." Jan surprised herself by cutting down her hours at work (although her kids were in school most of the hours) by going to church four times a week, by joining the choir (which she never enjoyed), by attending a Bible study class four hours a week during the hours she used to be at work, by baking a lot of bread, and giving up hunting. Later she recalled these events as if they were a dream. She said, "I felt like I had been hypnotized, like a character in a 1940's psychological thriller. I just stopped thinking, feeling or sensing my body."

Patrick disallowed any sexual experimentation, which had at one time been a delightful part of their marriage to Jan, and he would only have sex in "the missionary position," without foreplay. As the year moved along, Jan began to feel used and refused to have sex with him, about which he lectured her and berated her, though he never tried to force her.

Increasingly over the year, Patrick showed signs of ripening paranoia. He gave the television away, lecturing Jan and the kids about the "evils" of the television programming and the "secular way of life" that was portrayed on the screen. He read the Bible aloud after supper, keeping the kids stuck in their chairs for an hour or more while he harangued them with threatening interpretations of the texts. If either child complained, he threatened to "take off his belt." He said he was trying to teach them lessons they needed to meet the "harsh and depraved world." More and more, Patrick closed himself in his study room to pore over his Bible and other texts.

Jan was by nature an easygoing sort of person, a peacemaker, though in looking back on this time, she referred to herself as "a wimp." In time, she recognized that her husband was turning into a kind of "Christian monster." She found herself imagining living somewhere else, in a little house where she could live without the haranguing, the paranoia, the demands on her time and spirit. She had always been against divorce in the past, but surprised herself by finding less resistance to the possibility.

Jan made an appointment with the pastor, telling him only of her concerns about Patrick, not of her idea of leaving. Predictably, the pastor counseled patience, prayer and understanding, and also informed her of her duty to stand behind Patrick as her husband and the father of her children. Since she knew that this pastor had abetted Patrick in the position he was taking, Jan realized she could have expected no more than this, but we all hope to gain better understanding from someone.

Actually, Jan did try prayer, Bible reading and talking with some women in her group at church "behind Patrick's back." These attempts did nothing but help her see more clearly what influences Patrick was using to bury himself more deeply in his cave. Jan suggested marriage counseling, but this sparked predictable rage and haranguing from Patrick that the "problem" was Jan's "spiritual resistance."

Jan met a man at work, a man with whom she could talk. In a twist of irony, Patrick was right--her working was dangerous to their marriage because it allowed her to see the world outside the prison cage he was making for her at home.

Jan loved going to work.   She sold advertising for the newspaper, and met a lot of friendly and effectual people. Among them was Richard, the man who was to become a close friend.

What Richard saw, and what Jan recognized, was that Jan and her children were being poisoned by Patrick's regimenting and self-centered "Christianity." Much the opposite of being "saved," they were being "sacrificed" to Patrick's pathological Christianity, to his prejudices, paranoias, and political ideology.

Jan consulted a psychotherapist, essentially in her words, "to find out if I am crazy." To her good fortune, Jan found a good therapist who confirmed Jan's view of Patrick's behavior as harmful, terrorizing and diminishing to her value as well as that of the kids. With the therapist's help, Jan planned to leave Patrick.

When she asked Patrick to join her in a therapy session, to tell him of her decision, he was completely disoriented. He told her he didn't "have time," with his busy schedule at the church and work, to go to the therapist. He told Jan he "didn't believe" in marriage counseling anyway, since the true answer was prayer and Bible reading. Jan told him it was not marriage counseling at all, but her own individual session and she simply wanted him to join her to explain a few things. Patrick agreed to go, apparently with the belief that Jan had discovered that she "was the problem." He asked if the therapist was "a Christian," and Jan said she was, though she'd never asked.

Patrick took the news of Jan's leaving in absolute disbelief. He sat paralyzed in his chair for a few minutes, then began sobbing and repeating "how can you think of this? I have worked so hard to do all the things right that a Christian man is supposed to do. How can you think of this?" Then he moved on to several other positions, blaming the therapist for "putting the thought in my wife's mind," accusing Jan of having an affair or taking drugs, threatening Jan and telling her he was going to take her up "before the tribunal at the church." This latter procedure is one often practiced in evangelical churches today, which is that "sinners" such as "adulterers, women who have abortions, divorced people" and others are required to go up before the church, confess their sins and then have the congregation vote on whether they should be allowed to stay as a member of the church or not. In other words, people can be exiled for perceived "sins" after being humiliated in front of the church members confessing their "sins."

Jan refused to budge. She just calmly and strongly told him the reasons she was leaving, the incompatibility of her thinking, feeling and plans for the future with anything that had to do with Patrick's life. She said she hoped they could work out co-parenting in a way that was the best for the kids.

Patrick was aghast. He told her she could not do what she was planning because it "was against God's Law." He yelled at Jan and at the therapist. He cried. He begged Jan to reconsider, to have "Christian compassion" on him, to come home and be his wife again, to sleep with him like she should. Jan informed him that she expected him out of the house by nightfall and that as far as any physical contact was concerned, she was entirely nauseous at the thought of his ever touching her again. He bellowed at her, *I am a good Christian man and you will regret and grieve this before God!*

Jan had consulted an attorney, and dissolution papers were served on Patrick the next day. He was convinced that she would surrender her cause long before the divorce came through, but she did not. He could never believe that Jan would dream of following through with her decision. He sent her

Biblical passages each day, newsletters from his favorite Christian authors with reasons agains divorce, articles from *Christian Woman* exhorting patience, prayer and "grace." He set the pastor loose on her, and she hung up on him and closed the door gently but firmly in his face. The pastor and Patrick bemoaned the state of "modern woman," and the pastor said that in the old, more Christian days, a woman could be beaten for such behavior without mercy. Patrick even had two appointments with the therapist with the expressed purpose of "trying to understand Jan," but the not so hidden agenda of trying to "convince" the therapist to get Jan to change her mind.

Patrick simply could not believe that Jan would not "see the Christian truth," and relent her position. He sincerely saw himself as a "man of God," a spiritually advanced disciple of Jesus, a person with the keys to the Bible and a good man. He had never hit her, had provided well, had given her a good house to live in, had impregnated her, had tried very hard to show her the ways of the Lord, had "brought Christ into a formerly godless house." He never did and perhaps never will get that what he did was not to save Jan's soul but to temporarily steal, poison, wound and abuse her soul and psyche.

I wish I could say that such a story is rare, but it is not. With the backlash of the Pathological Christian Men's Movement, such men will become more prevalent, not less. Christian men are being schooled by the literature of this movement into greater narcissism, self-centeredness and negative patriarchy and away from the individual psychotherapy that so many men desperately need to have. Men have always hidden away in groups, in armies, in teams, in the priesthood, in all kinds of collective forms of avoidance of the work of individual and personal depth and of the bringing to consciousness their own shadow and archetypal material.

If any man is serious about developing his psyche and having a true intimacy with a woman, he will do the hard work of individual self-analysis by whatever means possible, each man to his own highest level of personal maturity. Then he will try to take this maturity and integrity and meet his equal in a woman, who must do her own self-analysis. Group work, support groups and the like, are valuable insofar as they may introduce the possibility of seeing normalcy in the variety of individual expression that can come from seeing other people struggle. Individual self-confrontation and personal responsibility, however, are the essence of developing a lasting and valuable integrity of psyche.

Pathological Christianity so dissuades men and women from personal maturity that it will be best to lay aside any and all "spiritual pursuits" *at least* until one's fiftieth birthday, if they ever expect to develop the capacity to think, feel and act with any sense of autonomy or integrity.

Double Standards

There is and has always been a double standard for men and women in Christianity. A Christian man can be brutal and rageful with a woman and it is defined as a "temper" as in the phrase, " he has a bad temper, but he is praying about it; he's a good Christian." If a woman is angry or even disagreeing with a man, she is considered to be "unfeminine." A little story from a popular evangelist's life (told by his wife) will illustrate this:

"Bill had a bunch of kids over for a Bible study. He was sitting in a big easy chair while the kids were sitting in other chairs and on the floor. I was sitting on an uncomfortable straight back chair, part of his 'class'. I got a funny image and said to the kids, 'look at the big old king on his throne!' The kids laughed, but he threw his Bible at me and stood up and barked, 'don't you ever speak to me that way again, woman!!' The kids brought him back the Bible and he started teaching again, they looked scared but very attentive to him. I think he was telling them about the Sermon on the Mount. I left the room, utterly humiliated. He never had any sense of humor about himself at all. He takes himself more seriously than Jesus or God and I think he actually believes he is more important than them."

Pathological Christianity is a male privilege psychology, a view of men as the primary dynamic operative, the prime movers of the world, and women as the servants of these prime movers.

What models for men do we see in the Bible (paying special attention to the "New Testament" and its prototypes for Christians)?

First, there is God, who is always referred to as He. This is not merely a linguistic accident, but a firm political conviction to establish and keep in place the message of male superiority. Now we might think that at least his adversary would be a woman, someone he could crush and boss around, but not even that role gets to be played by a female. Satan is "the other side," the competition. As God has dominion over all, Satan has permission to get his licks in on the earth, to try to win out and get souls for his own dark kingdom, to make them horrible and unrepentant sinners. So we see that both of the power positions are taken up by males, who are in control of the entire universe. There is not a single female in contention for a position of ultimate authority. Indeed in the Creation Story, the female is only an "after-thought."

The "Old Testament" patriarchs, such as Abraham and Solomon were universally wise, enduring and powerful. They made the right decisions and knew what was best for their people, they represented the highest standards. They were the idealizations of what it meant to have power and wisdom and it went without saying that this power and wisdom would be invested in men, not women.

If we can set aside the part of Jesus seen as God and focus on the model of Jesus as man, we can see a prototype for many of the problems that men have in relationships with women and with other men. We can also see the ideal that many American men--to their mishap--strive toward, that is, our ideal of the *hero*. Jesus was worshipped by his followers and scorned by his adversaries. He was seen as unique, powerful, mysterious and strong, strong enough to withstand anything with barely a whimper. He showed few emotions for one under extreme duress. He had a tremendous effect on other people, yet seemed to have no true friends. He was too distant, isolated and odd to have a true equal as a friend. He was highly idealized and vilified, but could never find a clear, true and enduring intimacy with a single other human being. He rejected his own mother when she tried to accompany him in his final days. He knew virtually nothing about his earthly father and apparently had almost nothing whatsoever to do with Joseph. He instead kept his attentions on his "heavenly father," his spiritual source. He was gifted in the extreme, yet ultimately cheerless, melancholy, alone. None of his disciples would stay awake with him all night before he was crucified. Could this be because they were disciples and not equals or friends? Jesus in his model has instructed two thousand years of Western men with a vision of the ultimate male life as one of giftedness, mysterious power, secret alliances, isolation, difference, uniqueness, separateness, relentless dedication to something "beyond" rather than what is present, a hierarchy of leading other men and managing them rather than equality with them.

If Jesus modeled a way of being that was difficult to understand for us who live on the earth and try to make our way through the mazes of relationships, friendships, work, play and death, and his Public Relations man, Paul, further exacerbated everything that tended to the pathological to an absolute fever.

We know that Paul was a fervent convert, an ex-persecutor of Christians who became deeply sold on his own understanding of Jesus as Christ. He devoted and consecrated his efforts the rest of his life to building a universal enterprise of the new religion. For whatever good he did in making Christianity known through the world, his insistence on the badness of life and the worthlessness of individual thought, feeling and action is the basis for Pathological Christianity as discussed throughout this book. Leaving aside whether you agree or disagree with his message or methods, we can see that as a model for men of how to live life he leaves us again with an image of the ideal man as grandiose but isolated, powerful but friendless, gifted but malcontent, unsettled, angry, insistent on his own righteousness, intolerant, hateful, competitive, woman-despising, living only for the *Company, the Corporation,* in his case, the new Professional Religion he was founding. Where does Paul help us know how to live in our intimacies with our friends and family, enjoying the natural world, animals, plants, the environment around us, or any of the things we can actually know. He lives and preaches an attitude and philosophy of other-worldliness, a perspective of hatred of body, world, woman, child and sensual delight. He is a denigrator of all natural joys and of simple pleasure. Is this not essentially what men are still taught--hatred of self, body, others, woman, nature? Professional psychotherapists see the evidence every day.

In order to avoid a long-winded discussion on each figure in the Bible as images of men and their model for ways of living and believing (Jesus's disciples, the apostles, Old Testament prophets, seers, Cain and Abel, etc.), I will only mention that a review of all the stories in the Bible show men (or male deities) as the prime instruments of active change, difference, meaning and accomplishment of purpose in the present world and any other world. This fact is common knowledge among thinking feminists today, but the consequences of such storytelling bears repeating in the context of Pathological Christian Psychology. The result of all these stories is a model for men of entitlement, of dominion over nature woman. The cost of the heroic aggrandizement, entitlement, power and grandiosity is isolation, loneliness, emptiness, lifelessness. Fortunately many men have begun to see that this "heroic" vision of men is not worth the cost. However, Pathological Christianity is going full strength, and gathering momentum once again in our culture and abroad, and one of its basic tenants is this view of men and women.

The models for women in Old and New Testament are primarily images of passivity, goodness in endurance, devotion to their men and "silence before the Lord." These, then, are the models adapted in Pathological Christianity for what is called "feminine." Confining ourselves primarily to New Testament models, our most compelling image is that of Mary, mother of Jesus. What do we know of her? Primarily that she is a "good person," by which it is meant that she is virginal, devoted and accepting of God's decision to use her as the vessel of his son. She humbly and gracefully accepts the gift, without asking any untoward questions. When Jesus arrives, she devotes herself to him with complete adoration, consecrating her entire life to his well-being, even after Jesus has rejected her. We can of course see something noble and valuable in a mother's devotion to her child, but it appears that she has no real other use in life. We learn nothing of substance about her relationship with Joseph, the cuckold, whom she tells, in essence, "get with the program." How many women become overly devoted to their children even when the children are clearly old enough to do better increasingly on their own? Is this not for many women simply a way of avoiding the conflicts, intensities, ecstasies and power that they might have to encounter if they developed themselves intellectually, took their husbands or male partners seriously, had a life of creativity and production? Mary's "goodness" comes from her acquiescence to the masculine, to God, Jesus, to the powers. Evangelical Christianity would like nothing better from women than that they would see Mary as a perfect model for the "Christian Woman."

Other women in the Christ story are also as two-dimensional as Mary mother of Jesus. Just to the same extent that she is good, perfect, the ultimate vessel of the light of the world, Mary Magdalene is sinful, guilty and a carrier of the darkness of woman. Magdalene is the prostitute, the only other model available to women in Pathological Christianity. She is bad because she is active, sensual, of this world. She is the body, woman's sexuality in action. Worry not, however, because by the end of the story, she has become repentant and devoted to Jesus, to the masculine "spirit-oriented" "other-world oriented" religion by conversion. In the end, she is as passive, sweet and devoted as Mary mother of Jesus.

These are the two main models of women in the New Testament. Woman is modeled as good, passive, devoted, sinful or guilty, depending on the amount to which she serves the man. A good woman is defined as one who is fawning over men, endlessly trying to do their bidding (perhaps reading endless articles in current magazines about "How to Make Your Marriage Work," and the like?) , reclining, withdrawing and "being silent before the Lord, serving others and never questioning or understanding her own value but only that of the "lord" she serves, worrying about her own adequacy. Woman, in Pathological Christianity cannot make things happen on her own, so if she tries, if she is efficient or powerful, she is "unfeminine."

The way "Christian" women have gotten around this prohibition to being *active,* is to be *eager, exuberant, cheerful, enthusiastic and endlessly aflame with the spirit of Jesus and in the service of Jesus.* It's a tightrope, but numerous women have been able to walk it. A "Christian" evangelical woman can be active in business, wealthy, powerful, but she must always portray herself as a *servant of Jesus.* As such, she must always "look feminine," be non-conflictual, graceful, ascribe all her accomplishments to "the Lord," not question the male hierarchy but learn how to use it to her benefit. She must learn to be sneaky, conniving, manipulative, controlling and always to portray herself as loving and spiritually motivated.

The net result of this paradoxical position for Pathological Christian women is that they are in the same trap as the men. They become isolated, lonely and intolerant. They are afraid, depressed, self-hating and cut-off. No man can be intimate with a woman who is *eager, exuberant, cheerful, enthusiastic and aflame with the spirit of Jesus.* She is utterly unavailable. She is unreal and living in some profound inauthenticity. Her soul and body have been annihilated by Pathological Christianity and its trance. The Impossible Commandments of Pathological Christianity are the source of eating disorders of all ilks, clinical depression, anxiety, loneliness and self-hatred in women. How can you have self regard or believe that you are something more than the mere vessel of men when you are taught to be exuberant, non-contentious and silent before the Lord (men)? How can you see self-worth when your only two models are to carry the male Christ child in silence and acceptance or to be a whore?

Men and women who wish to understand and love each other and themselves will need to realize that neither the Christ story nor any "spiritual" story will be adequate to the development of the kind of profound tolerance, passion and discovery that are possible for them individually and together. Pathological Christianity teaches a political model of social control of women and men to limit the sources of power, wealth and understanding to a small minority of people. All Professional Religions are forms of politics based on the current ruling power class's manipulations of personal acquisition of control and knowledge, and will always be cultural manifestations of their time and place. Pathological Christianity, the dominant world view of our times, teaches men entitlement, grandiosity and narcissism, isolation, competition and hatred of nature, other men and women. It teaches women self-hatred, purpose only in the service of men and "emoting" rather than feeling. It teaches women to be hysterical and sentimental as a way of covering up all "unacceptable" thoughts and feelings, such as anger and rage. It teaches women to worry about being a "Good Christian Woman," to worry about their man, rather than to think, feel and act maturely.

Money

Closely related to the question of worth linked to gender is that of worth linked to money and possessions. Since men control the wealth in the world, they also control the definition of personal worth. A capitalist assumption is that if you have money, you deserve it. This idea is the urchin of Calvinism which assumed that affluence was a sign of predestination, the sign of one chosen by God for the good things in life. For Pathological Christianity, cleanliness is next to godliness, but wealth *is* godliness. Large sums of money assure ownership of reality--the term is *real estate*--and that translates into ownership of Christ, ownership of the rights to fence off the world and take it into one's portfolio. *I am saved* means *I deserve* and that *all good things should flow unto me.*

Capitalism, the worship of money, is taught every day in our school system as a result of the confusion over God's grace embraced and taught by Pathological Christianity. Students do not learn or become intellectually deepened, because they are working for grades and not for learning, that is, for money rather than for character. If you give a high school student a choice between taking a challenging class in which he will likely earn a "C" and a boring, contentless class in which he can put an "A" on his transcript, he will take the boring class. If you give a college bound student a choice between a class which the desired (expensive, over-rated) school sees as favorable toward admission and one which he might like to take for his own interest, his parents and he will agree that he must take the "prep" class. It is too dangerous to risk poverty and insignificance by taking a classes that are not "college preparatory". What if your SAT scores are not very high, and your transcript contains several art and literature classes or god forbid some auto mechanics courses which you took because you thought it might be good to be able to work on your car yourself?

For men in particular, nothing compensates for lack of money.   A rich man, regardless of his ruthlessness or consumptive abuses or bigotry is held in the greatest esteem. A wise, compassionate, intelligent man who has no money is unfit and suspicious. A common question for such a man is, *if you are so smart, why ain't you rich?* Donald Trump was chosen man of the year by a high school in South Dakota and it turns out that the kids knew almost nothing about him except that he was filthy rich. When asked if there was anything wrong in Michael Jordan losing millions of dollars in gambling, rather than perhaps building a teen center in Sacramento, a high school student told me "it's his money and he worked hard for it. He deserves it because he is Michael Jordan and he can party it away filling Folsom Reservoir with Jack Daniels if he feels like it, just because he is so good."

The best mirror we have for Pathological Christianity's view of money is professional sports. The cherished athletes are *saviors*, so they are paid extravagant, gross and shameful amounts of money. They are our Christs. Through them we have grace, the outrageous entitlements of fame, fortune, privilege and money that Pathological Christianity instructs each of us to expect by the grace of Christ, if not in this life well then at least in the afterlife.

Pathological Christianity praises greed and acquisition as rightful and godly hunger--as long as they are practiced for the glory of God, in the name of the Lord. There is even a phrase among the evangels for one who is rich and famous through "Christian Ministry", that is "to be raised up by God." The phrase is used in this manner: "After I wrote that book, praise God, the Lord raised me up and a million people read the book and now here I am preaching in this stadium. Thanks be to God."

According to Pathological Christianity, the rule that money equals godliness only applies to Christians. Whenever a non-Christian earns a great deal of money somehow it is automatically an ungodly conspiracy. This is source of the Jewish pogroms through time.

When Marxists, Taoists or Jews earn big money, then money is evil, tainted with Satan. When Baghwan Shree Rajneesh had 16 Rolls Royces, the populous was outraged. When Ross Perot or Michael Jordan has enormous possessions we admire them.

Capitalism is associated with godliness. Other forms of government with ungodliness. Russian communism has been a good example of this through this century. It is not because the individual heart could not worship whatever it wanted, since it always can, but because money could not be poured into churches. Christianity was unprofitable in Russia, thus the rest of the world wanted capitalism. In capitalism, the principles of Pathological Christianity make the leaders rich. Capitalists worship money, thus are in step with Pathological Christianity.

Fundamentalism

This word is made of two parts, *fund* and *ment*. Fund refers to a stock of money, to a piece of land on the river bottom (which has the richest soil). All fundamentalisms are capitalisms. At their root is money, territory and acquisition. Wherever we see fundamentalism, we automatically see the urge to control land, territory and human souls. Fundamentalist Christianity does this by building little empires all over the map. At this writing, one of the large "Christian" organizations just built a new 400,000 square foot headquarters in Colorado Springs, and is hiring a thousand new people, at a time when the national and world economy is in serious jeopardy. Where is this wealth coming from? From people who are convinced that the world is coming apart at the seams and that these *saviors* will provide the only safety and haven. The *babies* want a little nest where they can go in the times of trouble.

Fundamentalists leaders have always depended on envy, greed and fear as essential human characteristics which can be converted into cash. They will always find a way to get the richest river bottom land, the most cash and the most acquisitions, merely by preying on those people who are most vulnerable.

A well-known ploy among some evangels is that of the "suffering savior." One well-known "suffering savior," we'll call him George, was in a bad automobile accident which left him disabled. There was controversy among doctors about whether he actually was disabled, since several could find no reason that he shouldn't walk, but George swears he cannot. Meanwhile, he has been carrying on a very profitable autoministry "serving the disabled in Christ's name." He writes and speaks and sends out a newsletter to serve those disabled in many ways. He talks to people with "disability problems" on the phone endlessly and prays for them over the wires. He has found a way to write "contribution letters" using his "disability" to make enormous profits. Many of his "contributors" are wealthy, guilty people who have a relative who is disabled. George's "river bottom," his fertile land is his disability. Because of this purported incapacity, he feels entitled to everything he can get while serving the poor and wretched of the earth, just like Christ. Many people consider him very "godly" and "inspiring," but he's actually quite a lady's man, to the chagrin of his wife, who does her best as a good Christian woman to ignore his peccadilloes.

He claims impotence after the accident, but there is some evidence it may be only at home.

Chapter 9. *Histories, Heavens and Hell's Bells*

THE AVERAGE AMERICAN EVANGELICAL Christian has no clue of the history of his or her *own* religion, nor even the dimmest information of the bright rainbow of other creeds and faiths held by people just as intelligent, visionary and serious as any Christian has ever been. Let's forgive one enormous ignorance, that of knowing other religions, since it would take a lifetime of serious effort and scholarship to even catch the light of a few of them. Of course the root of this ignorance is not lack of time or effort, but Pathological Christianity's assumption that nothing is worthwhile except its own cultic command and control. Pathological Christians are actually convinced that they are absolutely right and all other-thinking people that have ever lived are absolutely wrong. This is in the nature of fundamentalism, which always scorns and condemns the views of the dissenter or non-believer.

What is unpardonable is American Pathological Christianity's disregard of its own religious history, a recognition of its parenthood in other religions, even its plagiarism of other credos. Knowledge of predecessors and of the impossibility of original thought is humbling, since it dims one's belief in his or her exceptionalness. This is why Pathological Christianity cannot afford knowledge.

Pathological Christians would be paralyzed with astonishment if they had even a vague glimmer of what "good Christian proselytes" have wholeheartedly believed. Of course they would reject any creed but their own dull-witted gnarled formula, because to allow any unusual thought is to pave the way for the devil.

As a matter of fact, current language in Pathological Christianity even distinguishes between the evangelical club, to whom they refer as "Christians" and all other ways of thinking within Christendom through ages and places. I was astonished recently to hear someone refer to a Catholic priest as "a non-

Christian" despite the fact that if any protocol has a claim on the
name Christian it is Roman Catholicism.   This fellow even
informed me vehemently that Catholicism was *another religion*,
a "pagan religion" that had nothing to do with Christianity.

Pathological Christianity has disdained and ignored
Saints, the Holy Fathers of the Church, the endless and crucial
debate   about   the   Trinity,   Arianism,   Nestorianism,
Monophysitism, Monotheletism, all things concerned the relation
of Jesus Christ to God and man, the political history of the
Nicene Creed.   They are utterly ignorant of the discriminations
of Orthodox Eastern, Armenian, Coptic, Jacobite and Nestorian
Church.   Reformers such as the Dukhobors, the Christians of the
Universal Brotherhood held strictly to the equality of men before
God.   Their resistance to the state or other authority could teach
Pathological Christians a thing or two about spiritual power as
opposed to the rude practice of disseminating newsletters and
founding political organizations.   For over 250 years at its
earliest, Christianity was a martyr's religion, and persecutions
were official and legally sanctioned as a method to annihilate
Christians who refused to worship state and emperor.   The early
Christians were enemies of the state rather than bedfellows with
its drudges.

Most educated and uneducated Christians today think
that the Bible was always taken literally by properly believing
Christians. However, through the two millennia since Christ, a
wide wiggly line of possible interpretations of "Bible" has
wormed its way through history. Most third century Christian
ministers saw Bible as literary allegory of the human condition,
for example. Fathers of the early church with the stature of
Origen himself saw scripture as a kind of literary story about the
human experience. Tertullian referred to the Christian story as
"absurd" and said that he believed because it was absurd, that

was what convinced him. This is far different than banking on a concrete Divine Plan For History, with a specific Outcome.

Christians have held that Adam was a bisexual being, made of dew, soil, stones, angel-energy and grass, that he was a second angel, two hundred feet tall, and that his skull is the hill upon which Christ was sacrificed. They have believed that the sons of Cain were cannibals and witches and that they freely flew among the angels, nagging them. Many great Christians were also astrologers who saw no evil in astrology, since the stars and destiny were both creations and mysteries of God. They have seen the moon as a friend and as a demon. They have seen dragons, griffons, demons, angels, apparitions of the Virgin, and the Christ appearing. They have witnessed the New Jerusalem whose gates are angels, pearls and tribes of Israel. The Holy Sepulchre has been interpreted to be the *omphalos*, or the Navel of the World. The Cross, now empty of Christ, has been seen as the re-appearance of the Tree of Life from the Garden Paradise, and when Jesus got off it, he went down into Hell to harrow the place and fetch Adam and other patriarchs to relieve them of the dark suffering that they endured. Gnostic Christians held that nothing at all existed but dark and light which battled endlessly, and that all else was illusion. A moiety of this belief continues in America, where light (in the form of "lite") is equated with Good. The less color the better, so we have colorless cleaners and beer and soft drinks which will purify our body for spiritual renewal. It has been widely debated over the epochs, even in such literature as *Piers Plowman*, whether the conflict between Jesus and the demons was a setup, totally unfair play, in which Jesus had the upper hand from the beginning, and was only "playing" at suffering to dupe the devils--and even possibly to dupe man? Satan complains that he was not allowed fair rules by which to play for the soul of man. Joseph may be divorced, and were he and Mary ever married, or did her perpetual virginity disallow this? Are the brothers of Jesus from an illicit womb? Did Mary fornicate? Stories abound concerning the feats and sufferings and miracles ascribed to angels and the dark acts ascribed to enemies of the church or demons. This is not even mentioning the Grail , the odd miracles of Mother Seton in the U.S., St. Peter's upside down crucifixion, wide disputes on the material which the streets of Heaven are made of, Gehenna (the Lord's Bonfire), views on last-moment repentance, the dissemination of Christianity through peregrination, torture or imagination.

Historical Pathology is refusal to see how one's own thoughts, feelings and beliefs derive from those of other people and times. It is the refusal to see that one's own view is as crazy and idiosyncratic as those of every other person in time and just as humorous. We like to take ourselves seriously.

Pathological Christianity has the humourlessness to believe that the reason for its dissemination was its nobleness, tolerance and capacity to convince people. We see in history that the growth of ranks of Christians was due almost entirely to the securing of Roman power, roads, buildings, business and money, and today because it secures the same in American currency. The other reasons for the widespread practice of Christianity are covered in my sections on psychology, but in summary, Pathological Christianity assures its followers superiority, belonging, power over others and entitlement.

Pathological Christianity tries to freeze out change. It is an attempt to conquer death and personal oblivion by rejecting history. Its *savior* tries to be "ahistorical," to assure its *babies* that no boogie man of time will get them. By refusing to look at its own oddness, its own craziness, Pathological Christianity becomes incestual, cultic and ignorant of its pollution. Pollution is passing off your waste onto others without cleaning it up; it's keeping yourself clean by shucking your trash on others. Pathological Christianity tries to stay shiny by wiping itself with other religions, ideologies, people.

God made the world, the air, trees, water. One might think that a Christian, who regards the world as created of the Lord, might be environmentally conscious. The Lord, however, gave dominion of the world (including the body of woman) to man, to do with as he pleased, according to Genesis. Try to find a book entitled *Christian Environmentalism*. You can find Christian mechanics, Christian dentists, Christian tax consultants, but you will not find Christian environmentalists. This is because Pathological Christianity entitles its *babies* to void the earth, to clearcut, to "pave Paradise," to build steel and glass "churches", to capitalize the earth in the name of personal power. Since Jesus is my personal savior, I can bring sight to the blind or raise the dead. I am deified by my action, which is God's Will. God's world is eternally regenerative, an unending resource through Jesus Christ, so whatever I cut down, God will replace if he wants it so. Salvation has no limits, so I can do as I please, being saved. Also, the physical world is Satan's. God gave Satan the physical, to tempt man; it is a divine parlor game. In essence, when I cut a tree, dominate a woman or pave a field in the name of the Lord, I am showing my power over Satan. Christian Mini-Mall; Christian Night at Candlestick Park; Christian Businessmen's Organization; Christian Athletes. What matters is to usurp and cloud all other thoughts, words, emotions, trees, skies, activities, with the word *Christian*.

Heavens

We love to invent Heavens, which are the club where people we like get to have their own Private Property with a sign that says

No Trespassing
Violators Will Be Prosecuted
By God!
(Our Divine CEO, Founder, Social Chairman, et al)

If we live in desert climates, we make heavens that have rich springs and cool air. If we live in Seattle, we slow the rain down and hang out our shirt on the line in bright sunlight. If we are poor, there we have all we ever want; if we are rich but sad, there we have happiness without giving up our bank account. Heaven is where the right people get the inside secrets from the Secret Holder, share his best wine, eat at his table and are never dismissed for being boring or stupid. Heaven is the divine metaphor for sanctioning what we like, a way to arrogantly and defiantly impose our churlish taste on others and they'd better like it!

Divine "21": How to Get to Pathological Heaven

You get to heaven through seduction and sales. First, you must assume a God who is a sucker for a sweet line, who is dying to buy your gumbo. You are a clever character. You have discovered how to win, like the Las Vegas slugs who found the formula for winning at "21". You have exposed the mathematical craps of the heaven game. It is a matter of probabilities. You pray the right words. You have the right relationships. You give to the church. You hum the hymns. You accept Jesus Christ as Your Personal Savior and round up a few other folks to gambol to the same rhythms. God, being Simple, is not smart enough to create a mystery beyond the smart aleck conclusions of a few literalizing and untutored American evangelicals. These persons believe they have unlocked the 1-2-3 bolt of Heaven and have a clean trail to the right hand of the Lord, where they expect a pat and the spiritual equivalent of an untraceable Swiss Bank Account.

Pathological Heaven is a hide-and-seek game between God and humans. God, the Wizard of Oz, hides behind a translucent screen holding up a rule book which we can but dimly see. Of course we must try our hardest to read the message, because it is vital to our getting the good stuff in life and getting to Heaven. What we must see clearly we cannot. Why? Because we are *bad children*. But never mind, because there is a loophole.

1. God has the thing we need absolutely.
2. There is a way to get it, but it is locked behind a door with combinations.
3. You can get in (or be convinced that you can get in) by getting the combinations from the Bible.
4. Only a few (evangelists) know where these combinations are in the Bible or how to use them to open the doors.
5. If you make an error, get lost, forget the combination, tough deal! It is only the result of your ungratefulness and unprayerfulness that you goofed up: you were *willful.*
    You can win the lottery!!

Money lotteries are a product of Pathological Christianity, since they promise sudden, undeserved salvation from the prison of money, concern, the tedium of the job and the domination of the boss. Their popularity, despite the astronomical odds of any individual ticket purchaser winning, shows the strength of the salvation fantasy.

Older cultures do not have the same seduction about money as a stand-in for Heaven. An old Mexican man was selling a chair on the Streets of Xichatinango. An American businessman asked him how much it was. "Ten pesos." The businessman asked how much it would be for twenty five such chairs. "Fifteen pesos each." The American expressed shock and tried to explain the amount of profit that could be gained by selling twenty five chairs, and asked him why he charged more per chair in a lot of many chairs. "Can you imagine how boring and tedious it would be to make twenty-five chairs *all the same*," came the reply.

A United Parcel Service girl came to my house and delivered some seeds for the garden. She said she had taken a delivery to a jewelry store, and heard a worker there tell the owner, "Great, your diamonds arrived." The UPS girl said, "I might have been tempted if I knew they were diamonds, but I know where I am going when I die, if I don't foul up. There I will have something even better than diamonds." Pathological Christianity offers Heaven more as a reward for not doing bad than for any good.

The hope of Heaven is the hope of superiority. The word heaven comes from the Indo-European root word *hamr*, which means two things: "covering" as in a blanket (the sky), and the two curved pieces lying round the collar of a horse. Heaven is the hope of being covered, of remaining above the darkness, on top, visible to god and the company of all the other *risen*. Pathological Christianity's Heaven desire to maintain individual identity, to be uninterruptedly "cared for" by the perfect mother/father, who loves, rearwards, attends to each child perfectly. This is the fervent hope of *babies*.

It is also a yoke, and as such we note that *hamr* is also the root word for "shame" and "chemise". Sex always gets in there somewhere, and heaven is the place which covers our shame up, if we get in the yoke. If we are good domestic animals, we will cover our shame.

I lived in an area a few years ago where farms were being butchered to make way for the mindless slapdash of suburbs. One farmer held on, and his cows roamed near fences on the route of a school bus. A Christian Mother filed a petition for the farmer to be forced to put brassieres on the teats of his milk cows. She was terribly afraid that her children would be perverted and think of nothing but sex after they had seen the udder of a cow. She wanted the cow to wear a chemise to hide its shame.

The purpose of Pathological Heaven is to cover over our body, to clothe us anew in godly raiments where our humanity, our corporeal existence will be hidden, forgotten, excised.

Hell's Bells

Hell is the fear of the dark, the fear of being below, unseen, unrecognized and alone. It is the fear of being sent away from our parents, and having to fend entirely for ourselves, of being totally responsible for ourselves.

The word hell comes from a root which means to hide and conceal, and also which means "cell" or a hut, the cellar. Hell is merely "the dark place" or the unknown. "Bad people" are those we do not know, therefore those whom we see as condemnable to the place of Hell.

St. Brendon is said to have met Judas Iscariot. Judas told him that he is burning in hell like lead in a crucible, but he gets weekends and holidays off, apparently because he was a disciple, although a bad one. Those people we know, those things we know, cannot be hell to us in the way that the unknown are. We are more willing to condemn forever to an eternally burning hell a person from a vastly different culture than we.

In the imagery of Hell, it is usually underground, deep in the bowels of earth, but originally it was held to be far off in the West or the North. The greatest punishment in the old days was to be banished or exiled, not to be killed. Socrates chose to drink hemlock rather than leave his blessed Athens. Transgressions, those which are the most deeply punishable, are responded to by the cold shoulder of invisibility. Hell is to be sent to a place where you are not recognized. However, this image has lost much of its power for the American, since not a single American save perhaps one Hopi who still knows his sacred geography, belongs in any place. Americans either move or are the product of moving. What they have done is to compensate by making everything the same. Heaven is where you recognize everything, so we have strip malls, McDonalds, K-Marts, always the same, anonymous and reliable. We have counterbalanced hell by ripping away darkness, by cutting back all the places where unknown creatures may live, such as the salt marsh, the forest, the swamp. We landfill them with our trash and then build the neutral and flimsy coverings where nameless, featureless, mindless Americans can acquire the fatuous trash they require to fill their spectral homes to the brink so no Hell can enter.

Generally polar lands have Hells of ice, equatorial lands Hells of fire, since what we suffer in small measure we can only imagine intensified as the greatest agony. The American lacks imagination, so he can only see Hell as a land of talk show anxiety, as a place of mental agitation. He can only dimly shiver before a fantasy of intense sensation, power, inexplicability-- especially he fears the inexplicable. If he has to live without his electronic devices, to do things directly with his hands, he will never know how to live. His vision of hell is where nothing has an automatic function, but must be understood, takes time, requires thought, forbearance and, most terrible of all, *threatens boredom.* For the American, product of Pathological Christianity with its insistence on gain, acquisition, power, money and recognition, hell is...direct living. Hell is the absence of anything to gain; hell is existence in simplicity, without beer or television or internal combustion motors or shopping malls, without large-toothed and grand-orbed anorectic barren females on grocery store periodicals.

Apocalypses

Many world cultures have in their cycles of stories about the universe a vision of the end of time. Generally in these stories the world ends in a furious whirl of dreadful activity (often a great fire). There is ample evidence that those who get the worst torment in these endtimes are the people considered to be the enemy of the storytelling tribe. A god pays for the loyalty of his worshippers by punishing their enemy. The "enemy" often turns out to be the majority of humankind with the exception of the few truly faithful.

There is solid theory that the Revelation of St. John is a revenge (in time) on Rome for Roman abuse of Jews. It predicts the fall of Jerusalem to the Roman armies followed in due time by the collapse of the Roman Empire itself. It functions as a compensation and healing balance for hurts suffered by the Jews.

The early Greek Orphics and other often persecuted mystery religions held that a blessed state of immortality was a gift only for the select few, the instructed and initiated. Many of the world's cultures have awaited a great purifying fire which will cleanse the world of the bad and useless people.

The dragons and beasts referred to in Revelations are quite clearly recycled myth figures from older story cycles. In previous stories apocalyptic beasts, dragons, snakes and bird-women or fish-women brought about the fall of humankind. The beasts are messengers and enactors of the will of gods. Their purpose is to cleanse the world of evil and set it right.

Visions of an apocalypse are the psychological manifestation of desperation over the obvious injustices of the world. Because the good often suffer and the bad often do just fine, an apocalypse seems like a proper and just format for cleaning up the world and setting it right. It is one more example of psychological immaturity. Pathological Christianity offers a primitive form of revenge on those considered "bad" and compensation for suffering. It promises that the divine parent will clean up the house and set things right.

Eternity

Imagine in detail a great day you have had. Picture the events of that day. What did you do, how did you feel, what was the place you were in like?. Imagine that day continuing for four weeks. Try to picture it continuing for two months, a year, five years, ten years. If you are forty years old, imagine this as the only day you have ever had in your entire life so far, then see it as an event continuing from your great grandparent's birth to your death. That's only a little over 100 years. Would you be bored? Now do the same thing with the worst day of your life, repeating every day for over a hundred years. Wouldn't you acclimate?   Heaven and Hell in Pathological Christianity are based on two concepts: a line of time to a goal, which is eternity, and then changelessness from that moment on. Human beings cannot repeat without variation, nor will the soul hold still. Change and evolution are the only pattern which can describe our essence. Heaven and Hell are modeled on a good day and a bad day, that is all. They are absurd, nitwit concepts if they are conceived of as place, yet brilliant if they are taken as psychological metaphors. Heaven is what the individual soul knows and wishes for in increase. Hell is the unknown. When we pray, we should pray for Hell in the measure we can tolerate, since this is the way we *deepen,* and Heaven only in moderation, because although it refreshes us it soon stagnates. Heaven is a lake with no outlet; Hell pulls the plug.

Christian Psychology and Satanism

Christians have always been deeply fascinated with Satan, since he is the unconscious of God, God's bad brother, once God's favorite angel of light (Lucifer) and now the Prince of Darkness, of the flesh, of the world. Satan is far more interesting than God, since he is active, said to be here among us, energizing, adrenalized. Satan is Christ's tempter, thus he is the unlived aspect of Jesus, the side of Jesus that he did not live out in the world, that he felt required to deny and mortify and resist.

The story of Jesus would be totally incomplete without such figures as Satan, Pilate, Mary, Judas and many others, since what we call "Jesus" is Jesus in the context of his words, acts and interactions with others. Jesus could exist without the presence of Satan, but *Jesus Christ the Messiah* could not. Christ requires Satan for his dance.

A mature Christianity would realize the importance of all the figures in the Jesus story as part of a story of the human soul. Each character in the Bible is a reflection of some aspect of each Western person's psyche. A Christian Psychology would recognize that each figure needs some psychological recognition, none is to be excluded or slighted. The result would be a deepening and enlightening into the *entire* story of Testament rather than on valuing only specific parts of the story. A Christian should ask, how are Judas, Mary Magdalene, Paul, Lazarus, the soldier at the foot of the cross, cuckolded Joseph, Solomon, Job and others active in my own psyche; how are they part of my psychology, my "Christian Psychology"?

The existence of Satanic cults is primarily due to the inflexibility and rigidity of Pathological Christianity. When a group claims all light, truth, value and meaning, and enforces that with money, power and influence, inevitably it will cause a backlash. Pathological Christianity has rejected Satan along with any dark, unknown thoughts or feelings, and thus exiles an essential part of the psyche. When I claim that Jesus is all good and without guile and that Satan is all bad and without redemption, what happens is that Jesus becomes an evil figure for some people and Satan becomes attractive to others, because the nature of the human soul is to combine qualities and seek breadth and depth.

Pathological Christianity is Christianity stuck in fear and paranoia and will naturally result in the flowering of Satanism. There is little difference between the psychology of Evangelical Christianity and Satanism--as a matter of fact, they are bedfellows. They are both practiced to gain power, control, energy and influence for their followers, and both require submission of followers to their definitions of reality.

The criminal and violent acts of Satanism--murder of babies, emotional, physical and sexual torture of children, the use of blood--are symbols of what is unconscious in Christianity, and will remain forever unconscious unless Christianity can expand its psychology and find a way to integrate and understand these dark and bitter longings. Violence becomes an act rather than a feeling when people become desperate, hopeless and powerless. Pathological Christianity abets desperation by refusing to find a place for a tolerant and loving psychology in its canon and by refusing the value of other religions, values, and credos--and the individual psyche. When we pretend that evil is something *outside* of us, then it really does become something outside of us: outrage and injury will be acted out and acted upon. A Christian Psychology recognizes that all men and women are brothers and sisters, and not in the modern egotistical sense, but in the old sense of being totally and ultimately responsible for one's actions and *respecting the individuality* of each other person. A Christian Psychology recognizes that my responsibility is to get my own house in order and be prepared at all times to give a hand to others--but only if asked to do so, never as a missionizer.

Chapter 10.
The Spirituality of Direct Experience, By Any Name You Like
The End of <u>Theological Agoraphobia</u>

*How to Infiltrate Pathological Christianity
and find personal satisfaction and release from
the curse of feeling bad, feeling trapped, feeling "wrong"*

AGORAPHOBIA IS THE FEAR of going out of one's house, the dread of meeting others, which is accompanied by a dread of "something awful" happening if one were to venture outside of the comfortable, well-known confines of one's nest. It is a terrifying state of existence, in which one is paralyzed from the freedom to explore the world, to see interesting places or people or even to do the "ordinary" activities most people participate in with hardly a thought, such as grocery shopping, going to a movie, talking a walk in the neighborhood or meeting friends.

Theological Agoraphobia bears a strong resemblance to agoraphobia as defined by psychiatry, but is more insidious, subtle and widespread. It is a pathology which infects the hearts and minds of vast numbers of people, keeping them chained in anxiety and fear the way that agoraphobia does more visibly to people imprisoned in their house by terror.

Theological Agoraphobia is a state of being trapped by the assumptions, prejudices, warnings and infections of fundamentalisms, of any fundamentalism in general and of Pathological Christianity specifically. It is the fear of "coming out of doors" into the fresh air of thinking, feeling and acting in freedom. It is the fear of "challenging God," of being trapped by the passing fancies and the paranoias of current thought tyranny, such as that of Christian Evangelism in our day.

The best current treatment of choice for agoraphobia is a gradual program of desensitization to the generalized fears and anxieties of "being out," of meeting the world and bringing one's self into the open with a realistic (rather than fantasy-driven) appraisal of the world outside one's door. Treatment and cure for this crippling disorder demands courage, patience and perseverance by both patient and therapist, since either one may be tempted to give up in the face of a challenge to all the previous conditioning and assumptions held by the patient before the decision to come out into the world.

The parallel treatment for *theological agoraphobia* is also gradual desensitization and deprogramming also, a step-by-step process of courage on the part of the patient to look boldly at assumptions, conditioning, fears, anxieties and prejudices that she has built up over many years, accompanied by a belief that it is not sinful for a person to think and feel and deepen her wisdom, knowledge and identity. A psychotherapeutic treatment for theological agoraphobia is one which demonstrates *respect* for the patient's competence, innate capacity to think and feel and express in relative freedom his or her fundamental character rather than a false self created by Pathological Christianity.

Treatment for theological agoraphobia requires that the therapist herself be psychologically prepared to challenge her own cherished beliefs and assumptions and put them boldly and forthrightly on the table (or chopping block) right along with those of the patient or any others. It requires that the therapist show both *respect* and simultaneously *irreverence* toward the function of self-righteousness, "holiness", "spirituality" and other psychological "nest building" that people do to cope with and elevate their theological agoraphobia. This work demands humility on the part of the therapist, accompanied by a little outrageousness.

The attitude of a therapist may be something like, *I sure as heck don't know everything, and I certainly don't know what is right or perfect or good for this person in front of me, and I myself am always prepared to learn and deepen my understanding of what is right or good for me. I will try to reflect with honesty, clinical skill and carefulness, along with a little bit of irreverence, what he is saying to me, and ask or encourage him to question his assumptions or conditioning, so that he can think, feel and act in a way that is congruent with his true self, which is masked by a false self. My purpose is not to get locked in his nest with him, to join him in his theological agoraphobia, nor to lock him in my nest with me, but to help him examine and challenge his entrapment, while I on my own time and for my own benefit examine and challenge my entrapment. If I give counsel or advice, I realize that it is with tongue in cheek, since the purpose of counsel is only to provide a backdrop or boundary to which he can respond, certainly never to coerce him into a particular course of thought, feeling or action in his life.*

This attitude is the precise opposite of the unethical, arrogant and denigrating one of Pathological Christian Counselors. These "professionals" attempt to indoctrinate and politically govern and manage the "herd" into a set of precepts, "biblical principles," and fly-by-night principles drummed up out of their own anxieties, fears and misgivings; a set of "received, collective" rules and *theological agoraphobia.*

How to "Play Christian": little hints for all-too-serious psychotherapists

If a patient arrives and claims to be "a Christian" and is immovably rooted and unwilling to open up the door on her *theological agoraphobia*, respect it, as you would respect any other defense. Don't try to destroy it or force her to change in any way. If she asks you if you are a "Christian," *just say yes, amen,* since you are by the training of being a product of a school, society and government thoroughly infected with Pathological Christianity. If she insists to absurd lengths, requiring you to use "biblical principles" as part of your "therapeutic procedures," merely take your handy Bible out of its case, turn to a page at random, close your eyes and let your finger fall on a passage. Read the passage, giving your patient a knowing look, pause for a moment of silent prayer (in which you will be thinking of clinical history, diagnosis, or even praying for guidance if you like--it can't hurt!) then just go on about your own usual clinical work in the style that is best for you. Ask often if your patient has "prayed" about a certain topic, and what the Lord has told her. It is a fine way of getting the wisdom of the unconscious, or who knows, God's help, in guiding your therapy. Even more effective is to *believe wholeheartedly* , during the session, in the Pathological Christian agoraphobia, and just practice it, go along with it, just to see where it goes. Then in your time of clinical reflection later, when you write notes or think about the case, exercise ethical clinical judgment in thinking about the case, challenge your own assumptions and the effect that pathological conditioning has had on *you.* Get you your own self clear. Get your own thinking, feeling and acting *clear.* The most effective form of creative erosion of a patient's certainty (the true source of his distress, that is, his rigidity and inflexibility to really change), is to flow with the certainty in session, even emphasizing it, dramatically joining with the patient, in order to help him see for himself in the mirror of your own words and body language, the absurdity of his rigidity. Take an acting class if you can't do this work. Acting class should be required at all schools which train mental health professionals, since acting is the essence of what happens in psychotherapy in any case.

If you cannot (respectfully yet playfully) keep some irreverence toward your own cherished beliefs or holy personality, can you expect your patient to leave his nest and learn to fly?

What Pathological Christianity Cannot Tolerate

Logic

Logic is considered to be some sort of arch-enemy of Pathological Christianity, because using standards for careful or reasonable thinking promotes assuredness in one's own competence and intelligence. It is often held in disrepute in psychotherapy circles too as being "too heady." By this, I assume that some theorists are afraid that people might think for themselves, make up their own minds, rather than falling under the sway of the *charisma* of the psychotherapist. What is often considered to be the antithesis of logic, that is, *faith*, is not its opposite. Unquestioning faith in another or in "received" knowledge is indeed the opposite of logic, since logic demands thoughtfulness, and Pathological Christian Faith demands unthoughtfulness, that is, stupidification. An intelligent use of logic has a kind of faith in it which comes from strength, dialogue and trust in God, because it assumes that if we are wrong, God understands that we are doing our best to try to understand.

Let me give you an example of the use of logic over ignorant faith. The Swiss psychiatrist Carl Jung investigated all kinds of unusual phenomena, myths, fairy tales, dreams and visions that people have documented over the ages. He investigated them as "products of the psyche," which, since they were produced by people who can often be assumed to be honestly reporting their experiences, are worthy of inclusion in our understanding of human psychology. For example, the image or concept of God, since it is a spontaneously occurring product of the psyche which has arisen in one form or another in all cultures, is clearly something of strong importance to human beings, and thus part of their psychology. Dreams, visions, fairy tales and the like are also expressions or messages about the human psyche. It is not that they might be or are products "beyond the terrestrial" or mystical or divinely inspired that is of interest to Jung, but that they are what the human psyche produces, and therefore worthy of consideration, logical, thoughtful, careful study of their imagery, their consistency, their connection to various activities of human beings. We have no right either to view such products skeptically as merely "infantile" or weird, or to view them as "innately holy" or divine. Logic tells us that a combination of respect and skepticism, a scientific attitude of investigation, flexibility, and open-mindedness, will assure us of learning the most we can from such human expressions.

A close-minded attitude based on *theological agoraphobia* can have only the effect of ignorance, anxiety, fear and self-abnegation, and wars between peoples.

Depth Psychotherapy

Depth Psychotherapy and individual analytical psychology are profound challenges to Pathological Christianity. The goal of analytical psychology is, in general, the formation of a position of self-observation based on understanding and imagination, and on confrontation of one's illusions, fantasies, prejudices and collective ideals. Pathological Christianity promotes conformity, acceptance and a fear of being "abnormal;" when psychiatry purports to define "the normal," it can become its tool. Analytical therapy helps patients use their courage, intelligence and competence to find their personal maturity, that is, to face the fear of being "abnormal" or being trapped by any sort of label of the type growing from the root of Pathological Christianity. By focusing on a person's *individuation*, the discovery of one's innate character, fears, fantasies, assumptions and where these are influenced by collective thinking, analytical psychology helps the individual find his deepest strengths, competence and to befriend his own unconscious darkness and self-abnegation. It teaches that part of individuation is the capacity to work with, respect and understand the collective, the family, the society one is part of, but to recognize the limits of collective thinking and resist the temptation to "go up on the cross" and try to be a savior of culture or of others.

No-thing can "save" us, not groups, not societies, not institutions, not "rituals", not "the men's movement", not "Jesus", not "faith", not hard work, not "the cause." As long as we believe we can be "saved" we will wait for the miracle. Good psychotherapy teaches us to put away delusions and fantasies of salvation, and to come to our deepest challenge: to see ourselves naked of the clothing of collective and "received" opinions, and think and feel and act individually, responsibly, respectfully and irreverently.

Politics

All churches should pay corporate taxes like any other industry. God should pay taxes for all the advertising he gets in churches. We might reduce the national debt if we had a God Tax, that is a tax on all land, beliefs, missionizing, mesmerizing and fundamentalisms. *Eliminate all non-profit agencies, eliminate all welfare.* We have "sin taxes," but we should also have "holiness taxes." This would be a real separation of church and state.

Infiltrate schools, be a rascal, erode the certainty of evangelists. Rather than argue with fundamentalists, merely tax them more. Expose elements of Pathological Christianity in print, on the radio, on television. Disseminate this book.

Recovery from Fundamentalisms

There are quite a number of things that you can do to end your *theological agoraphobia* and to begin to move in the world as a live being rather than an automaton. The first ingredient is to make a private and individual decision to do so, and then, decide when to begin speaking to your closest and most trusted friends or therapist of your decision. *Stay the hell away from groups for a while, keep your thinking and feeling secret. Guard, nourish and grow it in a hidden garden, for your own pleasure and nourishment.*

Much of recent "pop" psychology (another of the many hidden and ubiquitous forms of Pathological Christianity, the metaphysic of jackpot salvations, thinning diets and the like), has hammered the fundamentalism of "talking it out." The catchword of this current bubble of consciousness is "talk it out," as if yakking away endlessly heals. Certainly talking earnestly and intimately, and expressing heartfelt emotions with those near in kin or love with you are important. When there is harm or danger to you or others, you must take the responsibility to call for help, whether from police, social service agencies or whomever. But that is not what I am talking about.

I am saying, don't blubber, yack and spill your guts for the release or for the hope of salvation. Keep your own soul quite secret as a treasure and guard carefully with whom you share your deepest source of personal wealth. Stay away from **all** "movements" and all churches until you have made up your own mind, thought and felt your way into the issues involved. Then, perhaps, it is time to join in from the position of your own solidity.

Stay away from charismatic leaders, motivational speakers and workshops on making yourself better. Stay away from hypnosis since, though it is effective in symptom reduction, it poo-poos the profound importance of conscious thinking and integration of images, thoughts and feelings. Letting others "motivate" you or "hypnotize" you is quite akin, psychologically, to having sex with them, since you are opening up something that is the most intimate part of your being--far more intimate than your genitals--to the influence of people who are very likely getting their jollies on controlling the thoughts, feelings and actions of others. We know and read increasingly in the media how often charismatic leaders end up having sex with a "parishioner." *Don't sit on the priest's lap; remember he doesn't get much licit sex.*

Don't depend on Hollywood or television as your source of information about the human soul. It seems absurd to say this, because it implies the crazy fantasy that people *do this.* The amount of television or movies or video rental images that the average American watches is staggering. If you choose to spend your time and energy breathing this collective phantasmagoria, remember that images are stored in psyche *forever*. Is a gory or inane or insipid movie or situation comedy actually what you wish stored in the "library" of your soul, never to be erased? You can't give away your stored images or those of your children to Goodwill when you wish to be rid of them, they have a permanent, indelible effect on you.

A truly anarchical act in America today is to read the classic authors, the Greeks, the Romans. There is more depth in a sentence of Seneca than in the entire NBC fall lineup. And no commercials.

Talk To Your Parents Like an Adult

Apparently one of the hardest things adult human beings do is to speak to their parents and tell them in reasonable, rational, thoughtful terms what they are thinking and feeling. I say "apparently" since in years of clinical practice and discussion with friends and colleagues, I have rarely come across an individual who describes having that most basic and essential experiences of having moved into being a peer with his or her parents.

Let's try this out, something a little different for a change. *The goal of raising children is to get done with it. The measure of good parenthood is when it disappears.* We've been stuck with the trap of seeing parenthood as a lifelong pursuit. Rather than this, let's make a time for parents and children to retire from these roles!

Trish is 43 years old. Her daughter is 18 and just about to go off to college. Trish is terrified because when her daughter leaves, she'll be alone with "him," her husband, and never having gotten any training or college education, she's going to have to "start over." She "got away from home" by getting married to a guy she didn't even like, but her mother has always "ruled" her by telling her every step of the way what she should do about her husband, her kids, everything.. She's never had anything of her own, except her four children. Now the baby is getting ready to leave. So she hangs on tight to her daughter, trying to "squeeze the last drop" out of her daughter's life, overprotecting her and "loving her to death." Trish is afraid of her daughter leaving because she herself never grew up. Even today, she gets paralyzed and regressed in the presence of her own mother. I tell her she is going to have to "leave home," that is, to get a life and thoughts and feelings and actions of her own rather than doing what her mother consciously or unconsciously tells her to do. She is afraid that she'd "devastate" her mother by speaking up to her, by having her own thoughts, by contradicting her or refusing to do what she says. Ironically, she feels she'd "devastate" the very person who has utterly ruled Trish with an iron hand since the day she was born. For her own sake, for the sake of her daughter, and even for the sake of her mother, Trish needs to stand up to her, take a stand, get a life, begin to take charge of her own life, become an adult.

Pathological Christianity demands that people remain babies in order to "get heaven." All Trish is getting by remaining a baby is hell. I wonder if she will die with her diapers on, or if she'll get "potty trained." The Sacred Cow, "Parenthood," is sacred only as long as children remain very young. When the children grow up, parents and kids need to burn the diapers and hang up the crib as an interesting memento. Too many parents hang on to the position, "I am the parent," in order to keep themselves too busy to think, feel or grow up. *Being a human being is such a terrible burden! It is far easier to be a "parent" or a "child" or an "adult child of alcoholic parents" or a "Christian."*

Spend time in nature

Hike, swim, fish, camp, bird-watch, sketch scenes; observe nature.   If that will not interrupt your theological agoraphobia, what will? Observation of the variety, complexity, of the movements and beauty in nature, such activities have for all of time awakened in human beings feelings of awe and wonder. Unfortunately, what the majority of people have done with that awe and wonder is to try to nail it down, to make it manageable and controllable.   Since a tolerant and mature humility before nature is hard to maintain, because it means that we are simply a minuscule part of the whole picture, people have drummed up all sorts of laws, principles and concepts to aggrandize human beings, to portray them as having control over nature, answers to questions which are unanswerable. Pathological Christianity is a kind of *machismo* before nature, a strutting to make self feel important. But exactly like machismo, it is fake, easily destroyed, narcissistic and infantile.

Sexuality & Luxuriating Your Body

Sex and sensuality are not bad. They are good.

Marriage is irrelevant to sex, Christ or spirituality. The purpose of marriage is to produce conformity and reduce our anxiety, not to promote deep satisfaction in life. It is a legal arrangement that makes it easier for the state to trace people who are being anarchical. It is a way to produce the fantasy of *permanence, salvation, finality and transcendence.* The problem is that the psyche recognizes no legal arrangements, but works independently. Love, desire, passion, imagery and emotion come of their own accord. When you try to trap them like butterflies on pins stuck into foam board, all you have is stiff dead butterflies, colorless. True marriage is in the soul.

When people act on compulsions to have sex with as many people as they can, they are simply nervous Pathological Christians, trying to deny their heritage. Pornography is simply the shadow of piety.

When people try to stuff their sexual energy in the dresser drawer of the Church, it gets moldy.

When you have sex, go boldly and lovingly and kick St. Paul out. Enjoy the body, not in "rebellion" to the church; simply dismiss Pathological Christianity and put it out in the rubbish can with old Paul. St.Paul is nervous in the bedroom, he's a premature ejaculator, he can't get an erection, he spits and fumes. He is no fun at all in the sack, so stop inviting him in. The more you conform to his view of sex as "fornication," the more pornographic visions you will see. It is titillating to speak of and imagine "forbidden sex." Do you really need "forbidden sex" as a turn-on?

People engage in harmful, sado-masochistic sexual practices because they are not raised in freedom and honesty. Natural passion is delight and play and orgasm. It happens when people are raised to be people rather than neurosis-ridden compulsives. The "rules" of Pathological Christianity are simply perversions and exaggerations of our natural desires to be with one we love. This needn't be turned into a law, as we can see among the geese and the swans. They have no "ten commandments" but they follow the sweet path of attachment to one another.

A statement of Pathological Christianity is that sex is sacred. Does this mean that it needs to be sucked dry of passion, of Eros? No. The "sacredness" has nothing to do with a particular legal definition, i.e., Marriage. It has to do with the uniting of powerful unconscious urges and archetypal images that take place during sex. Committed and monogamous relationships? Sure, it seems best for most humans; but why kill it with guilt, self-abnegation, prayer, worry? "Affairs" are products of the dishonesty that is required by Pathological Christianity, since one cannot disturb the "ideal" image of the Christian Couple by facing the actual fact of psychological intensity, rage, the needs for privacy, by....psychotherapy!

Study the Old Philosophers

Study of the old philosophers makes you humble, especially of the pre-Socratic, those Greek thinkers who lived before Plato and Aristotle, who made philosophy neurotic, charged with political correctness, the marshaling of forces and conformity: they started *schools and institutions.* Forget the new philosophers--they are under the influence of Pathological Christianity, and are stingy and neurotic. They are members of Academia.

The old Chinese thinkers will blow your mind. If you spend some time with the *Tao Te Ching,* you'll read the heavy, dark, mean, whining, neurotic verses of the Bible and just about puke.

You will discover through looking into these old fellows that other people can and do think and that just because their thinking is not just like yours does not mean it is not deeply valuable. Broad reading in the old philosophy is never a waste of time.

Practice a form of art: painting, ceramics: beauty heals

It is a joy to do a piece of art which has only the purpose of representing some lovely vision or perspective. Beauty heals all by itself and making a pot makes Pathological Christianity irrelevant. True Art is sensual experience and speaks to all the little crevices in the psyche where Pathological Christianity dares not tread, all those places that ministers warn us not to go, because the devil lurks there.

Touching the forms and the materials awakens the body and shuts off the part of the mind that makes us fantasize that we need *salvation.* Salvation actually occurs when you make a piece of art, and is no longer a future or conceptual thing. That's why art is so dangerous to religions, even to the extent that a "Commandment" is that we should have no graven images of "God" or others. God is afraid of our individuality and personal enjoyment; he sure is *threatened.*

When you make art from your own soul, the danger is that you simply move into transcendence and there is nothing your neighborhood evangelist can do about it. You are simply unreachable, unteachable, un-*save-able*! You are one lost puppy as far as Pathological Christianity goes. I highly recommend it.

We know that art (from studies related to art therapy}opens up new neural pathways, new ways of thinking, feeling and relating to others and to the natural world. Doing art is extremely dangerous, because it can lead to *individuality.*

Develop Critical Thinking and Critical Feeling

A fine way to defeat Pathological Christianity is to read widely and indiscriminately. Pick up anything and everything and just read it. As you go, you will begin to develop those qualities most dangerous to Pathological Christianity, critical thinking and critical feeling. Infiltrating Pathological Christianity effectively requires that we emphasize and appreciate and develop critical thinking and critical feeling. How?

- Wide, random reading. Just go into a used book store or the Salvation Army and grab a few books on different topics---poetry, military history, carpentry, biography--and read them.
- Wide associations. Talk to people who are interested in a variety of things. Don't just associate with people like you--work associates or neighbors. Get to know people of a wide spectrum of ages, from kids to very old people.
- Do art. Doing art develops critical feeling, especially original art, because it challenges your whole brain and engages your body as well. You develop appreciation for form, nature, imagery and aesthetic senses.
- Psychotherapy: Good psychotherapy emphasizes critical thinking and critical feeling. Good psychotherapy does not just kowtow to the expression of emotions or to uncritical acceptance of oneself or of so-called "self-esteem", but emphasizes good critical thinking about self, theorizing and understanding of self in family and in society. Good psychotherapy emphasizes critical feeling, that is, it always promotes taking responsibility for your own thoughts, emotions and behaviors, and not dumping them on other people. Good psychotherapy promotes analysis of self, physical well-being, emotional freedom, social tolerance

and social action. Therefore, I exclude most forms of hypnosis, spirituality, massage, biofeedback, meditation or other trance-forming activities from the category of psychotherapy. These are good and important activities in themselves, but they do not promote critical thinking or critical feeling. They can be adjuncts to psychotherapy, but the real work of personal development is self-examination, confrontation of self, and acting authentically on the basis of these insights.

Study the History of Your Own Cherished Prejudices

Study the history of your fundamentalism. If it be Christianity, learn the history and the mythology. All of us are under the sway of some form of fundamentalism. Where you notice your own fundamentalism is where you are righteous or certain about anything.

It is astonishing how few "Christians" know anything at all about the history of Christianity, or even the history of the private, narrow sect to which they belong. They act as if their religion had always existed, in its present puny form, that everyone had believed in their own way, etc. Once you have studied the variety of ideas, beliefs, the incredible cultural variations of something like "Christianity," you'll never be able to take any American Evangelist one hundred percent seriously again. You will see that he is simply a variation on an old theme. It is the theme that counts, not the rules or private imagery drummed up for a particular age. This is why someone like David Miller, Professor at Syracuse University, entitled a book about the many facets of Christ with the title *Christs.* That plural form deeply enriches our vision.

Look at your life as a story rather than as an example

When you see that your life is a story, like a novel, and that you are simply alive to create another interesting variation on the theme of "humans," it takes away the impossible responsibility of "saving the whole world." Refuse to save the whole world, or if you decide to do so, at least do so realizing that you are a clown.

Life is not a concept or a precept or a principle. It is not a Plan, it is a story.

Challenge All Leaders

There is never any reason to accept without challenge anything anyone says, including this statement. Of the things I have said in this book, what have you challenged and not challenged? Question everything, make all leaders "guilty until proven innocent".

- **subterfuge authority**
- **do your own thinking and feeling**

Chapter ll. **Raise Your Kids In Freedom**

MANY PEOPLE THINK WITH DREAD about the prospect of raising children, or of making decisions in general, without some clearly defined system upon which to base their decisions. They can't conceive of consulting their own authority in resolving moral dilemmas nor in childrearing. They've been cowed by "experts" into believing that raising children is an awesomely complex responsibility that someone should not do without at least one graduate degree in developmental psychology. It is a reasonable fear and one that's quite understandable, since we have all been suckled in the bosom and tutelage of Pathological Christianity to doubt our own judgment, our own capacity to think, feel and behave responsibly.

Schools, teachers, parents and the political institutions are all agents of Pathological Christianity, wittingly or unwittingly. The last thing they would ever want is for their citizenry to be thinking independently of the collective standards or "norms." We are schooled in fear. We are trained from the moment of birth to mistrust private judgment, to work hard to eliminate our own "rebelliousness" against parents, against established institutions, against the *good society*. Often what is called "rebelliousness" is merely the natural curiosity of intellect, of imagination, of creativity.

The argument is often made that people thinking for themselves are unreliable, untrustworthy, and need a guiding set of principles, some "higher power," some higher capacity for decision-making, something beyond their own intelligence. Research studies may be cited ad infinitum that demonstrate that people who live without certain restricting and controlling principles are prone to crime or chaos or wildness. I think of this as the *Lord of the Flies* argument.

Lord of the Flies, as you will remember, is a book by William Golding, in which a group of boys is shipwrecked on an island where, without adult supervision, they become violent, abusive, tyrannical, cruel, mean, unjust and arbitrary.   One conclusion from this story is that the human being is naturally savage and needs restriction and control: civilization.   But the opposite argument holds up just as well.   These boys came out of a society in which they were never trained to think for themselves, to use their own internal ethical sense to work out problems of justice on their own, but instead were instructed and schooled that they were *incapable* of making their own decisions, that they had no judgment, that they were fools and savage animals who needed civilizing and training.   Is it any wonder that when adult restraints are lifted, the boys begin to act as they do?

I remember being in Spain in the 1970's, once in 1971 while Franco was still alive and once in 1975, after the death of Franco.   Generalisimo Franco had ruled Spain as absolute dictator, the one European fascist dictator in this century whose success in his country had been total and enduring.   He had ruled Spain in total autocracy, from an unquestioned position of Christian Fascism, of Pathological Christianity.

I admit having a certain comfort, a strange, nervous comfort, a feeling of nervous safety, and having some kind of eerie respect for the way Madrid was run in 1970.   There was, in effect, no crime, except, of course, that committed by the government.   One could be on the streets safely at night.   Doors could be left open.   Rape was almost unheard of (perhaps it was going on nightly, but the news didn't carry it: perhaps part of the attitude that "rape" was merely "sex").   Nobody dared take drugs, possess them or sell them.   There were no lewd or lascivious actions in the streets, no strip joints, no naked or nearly naked hookers hanging around on the street corners, not even kids kissing or petting in the alley ways.

Divorce, abandonment of children, violence in the streets, car theft, pornography, the kinds of things that people in cities today take for granted, existed hardly at all among the populous. Young women and teenagers were safe to walk the streets at 2 a.m. But there was always just around the corner, at least a couple of members of the *Guardia Civil* on the beat along the sidewalks.

The *Guardia Civil* was the state police. They dressed in tight uniforms with patent leather hats and carried machine guns. *Nobody messed with them.* Nobody messed with them because it was universally understood that if these guys arrested you for an infraction, no matter how small or insignificant, you became, in effect, their property, incommunicado from the rest of the world. It was not on the streets that the rapes, beatings, exquisite tortures took place, but in the interrogation rooms of the *Guardia Civil.*

These fellows had absolute freedom to rape women or to burn their nipples with lit cigarettes, to fix hot electrical wires on the testicles of men or crush their privates in a vise, to make teenage girls strip down in front of them and hold still while the *Guardia Civil* would body-search the cavities of the girls for drugs or whatever other trumped up excuse they happened to fabricate at the moment.

These police, under direct permission from the *Generalisimo*, had the right to take any measures they wished against any citizen they suspected of a crime in the wide swath of illegal activities outlined by the state in those days in Spain.

I mention this situation in Spain in the context of this book primarily because it is the most blatant and overt case I have seen of Pathological Christianity given free and total reign on a large scale. All subtlety of pathological conditioning was gone. Franco claimed openly and without guile that each day he ruled Spain was for Christ, for the Glory of God and for the Church. He made no bones about the fact that he found the ordinary citizen incapable of making his own decisions (I use the pronoun "he" because "she" as a decision-maker was utterly out of the question) or distinguishing right from wrong. To this end, he tortured, executed, exiled, harassed, humiliated and shamed any artist who brought what he and "the Church" considered to be "filth," "obscenity" or even a challenge to his unconditional rule. Any small hint of dissension was snuffed out instantly.

This is the ultimate picture of the rule of the Religious Right. Pathological Christianity in control. A citizen makes no act without consulting the state for the correct, prescribed and pre-scripted definition and procedure for determining right and wrong, that is, the institution or state or church-run thought police.

The next time I returned to Spain was in 1975, just after Franco had died. Everything in Spain had "opened up" and there was chaos in the streets, in government institutions, in the church, in every activity. People looked confused, anxious, and yes, excited. Things had fallen apart in Spain. Now it was dangerous on the streets. You didn't leave things unlocked. Every kiosk featured pornography. Rampant criticisms of the government flourished.

In the first free elections since Franco had bombed and murdered his way into power in 1939, there were dozens of political parties vying for power. Those who supported the "old days," the Franco days, were very quick to explain that this "insanity, danger, destruction" was exactly what Franco had predicted if people were given power. They would not know how to use it. They would abuse their power, and crime, pornography, perversion and chaos would run rampant in the streets. People would be confused and not know what moves to make.

It is true, people were confused and didn't know what to do. It was not, however, because they lacked the capacity to do so. It was because people in the height of what would be their maturity, in their forties and fifties, had never, for a day in their lives, been given an opportunity to think, feel or act on the basis of their own judgment and wisdom. They had been trained and conditioned into an absolute stupidity. When the doors of their prison were open, they had no training or experience in living or thinking as citizens rather than slaves of church and state. Naturally, they went wild and exploded in their freedom.

The adults went to the voting polls, most of them, for the first time in their lives. They wept and shook, weren't sure what to do. They were afraid and mistrusted the process. Many people feared that the election was a farce and that their names were being taken down for future incarceration or torture for participating in the elections.

They exercised poor judgment and were naive. They were suckers for every product that came out of the U.S. or other countries. They had been denied a lot of modern conveniences which were considered "decadent." They reminded me of kids I had met at University the freshman year who had grown up in extremely strict homes where the parents "protected them" from all sorts of "dangers" by ignoring or simply not talking about supposedly dirty or unacceptable topics.

These kids almost without fail went wild in college. They had to try everything. They kind of dropped off here and there, flailing their way into drugs and sex and alcohol. They had to experiment with everything. The legal drinking age was 18 and many of these kids bought up alcohol like mad and went straight to hell on booze. They had no training no experience and no model in the moderate use of these substances. They were not inoculated to survive in the world, but had been kept in a kind of "bubble" existence, shut off from infection, so that the minute they were exposed to the various "infections" in the world, they quickly caught every "disease." They had no protection.

What we are obliged to do for our children and for our citizens in general is just the opposite of this. An alternative to raising children in fear and control, an alternative to Pathological Christian Conditioning, is to raise children in freedom and love. I am not talking about permissiveness, but freedom. There is a huge difference, as I will explain. It is a lot more difficult than using simple-minded precepts, black and white discipline and the like, or on the other hand, simply letting kids run wild. It is hard work, intelligent and creative work, and I must admit that for many parents, is an impossible request.

For some people, those lucky enough to be raised in freedom themselves or those who had the courage to develop psychologically through personal effort, mentoring or good quality psychotherapy, education and travel, and who recognize the value of individual freedom, nothing of what I say will be shocking, but will seem natural and comfortable to them.

By raising children in freedom, I mean raising them in increasing freedom. The goal of raising children is gently guiding and encouraging them toward being autonomous and mature adults, peers (at least) of their parents, and totally free to think, feel and act on their own recognizance. Such a concept is hair-raising, utterly terrifying to those cowardly parents who hide behind the skirts of Pathological Christianity.

What begins as a mostly one-sided relationship of power in infancy, with parents directing, guiding and setting rules should from the very beginning have as its goal a peer relationship of compassionate adult years hence. Even when children are infants, the parents should recognize that in small but consistent, accumulating ways, they are beginning to communicate to their children whether it is their hope and goal for the child one day to be a respected equal with them, or whether the parents are looking to mold obedient, docile, mindless recipients of the parents' own frustrations, misgivings and regrets over lost opportunity.

At a very early age a child understands whether she is to be regarded as a person or as a kind of "antidepressant drug" for the parents, whether as a free and autonomous individual or a tool for parents to measure their own self-worth. Fundamentalists use the conformity of their children to convince themselves of the value of their beliefs. They think, in essence, *if only this child will meet the ideal I have set, if he will embody this fantasy, then it will make it true, and I can believe.* This is an evil use of children.

From the perspective of religions or "spiritual beliefs," it is very easy to know whether you are using children to buttress your own shaky beliefs. Are you imparting to the child the best and fullest information you can find about other points of view? Are you presenting these other perspectives honestly, thoughtfully, showing tolerance and acceptance and humility about your own judgment? Are you yourself willing honestly to question your cherished beliefs, put them to the same standards by which you judge other beliefs? Are you straightforwardly and with integrity attempting to incorporate what you learn of other beliefs, doctrines or points of view into your own?

This does not mean eliminating or shattering your own beliefs. It is, rather, an attitude of honesty with yourself that you are willing to consider that there may be many ways beyond your own narrow field of focus for people to achieve deep satisfaction and value in life.   In fact, no one person can know even a modicum of the answers to the important questions.

Give your own soul a chance and push yourself to an attitude of acceptance to learn new ways of thinking, feeling and acting.   Exploring what you can about other perspectives directly parallels what you are asking your child to do. You are asking him to give *your* ways of thinking, feeling and acting a chance; you are asking him to respect and tolerate your judgment, and you don't really know if it is something of value or your own, narrow nonsense.

Your attitude of love and acceptance toward your own soul will directly reflect how you see your children, how they see you and in some ways how they see themselves. Do you wish for them to have the same experience of permanently feeling bad, guilty and suffering you do? Or would it be your wish for them to feel good, accepted, competent, self-respecting, tolerant and compassionate towards others?

If you can treat yourself with respect, a little humility, irreverence and a sense of humor, if you can see yourself a little ironically and yet lovingly and not take yourself too seriously, your children will know that they have a chance to be people in your presence and not merely to perform roles like trained animals for your benefit.

Teach your children values from other religions and other cultures. Tell them stories from other traditions, give them some introduction to music of other cultures, introduce phrases from other languages. *Go into this lightly and gently.* Try to make your interest in other views something of fun and enjoyment, not a new form of Pathological Christianity, a new "missionizing".   Kids love learning new things, and have a natural curiosity that is absolutely killed by heaviness or "goals."

All this means you are going to have to do some homework. *Get busy!* Stop being so lazy and tired, and begin looking into literature, stories, myths. Open your own mind. Wake up.

How can you expect your children to do their homework, if you won't do yours? If your child reaches high school and will not do her homework, it may be because you are not doing yours. Think whether you have been open and curious and interested. What new ideas, what new form of self-expression have you looked into recently? What are you reading? What talent have you let get dusty in the garage? (By the way, how can you expect your mate or your friends to stay interested in you if you are *boring?*)

If you are unwilling to remain flexible, grow intellectually and work on your creativity, how can you possibly expect your child to do so? If you are growing progressively *stupid*, why should your children believe that you want them to become intelligent? So they can become stupid later in life like many adults they see?

If you teach your children *honor thy father and thy mother,* a well-known biblical principle, and you don't demonstrate tolerance and compassion to other people, curiosity about your own psyche and a desire to learn new ideas, the children might well *honor* you by becoming as closed and passive as you are.

Reading the Bible

I spoke earlier about a *Christian Psychology,* one which honors Christ and the Christ story. I spoke of how *all* the characters in this story portray for us a vivid and powerful story of the human soul and of human psychology. I said that this Christian Psychology is focused on the depth and development of the psyche rather than on precepts and principles. My mother always said, attract bees with honey, not vinegar. We keep using vinegar and trying to force people to drink it.

Pathological conditioning is bitter, acid, harmful. Yet if it is the only thing you have to drink, eventually you'll learn to accustom to it and even pretend to like. Of course, you'll expect others (particularly children) to like it and even ask for it.

The *Christian Psychology* I describe is one which, I hope, is closer to Christ than to Paul, one which invites people and recognizes fear, darkness and suffering as well as excitement, sensuality and love as natural. The Christ story has many forms, and the one portrayed in the Bible is an honored version of it--one among many. Some people will find other stories, such as the Buddha story, more appealing to their natures, more valuable for their own psyche. This is what maturity and psychological autonomy is about, the capacity to choose competently and boldly what is right for his or her own soul.

If the Christ story speaks to a person, and he chooses it and goes deeply into it, it will be a choice made from freedom and strength, rather that one out of fear, received judgment and lack of confidence. In the hysteria that Pathological Christians manifest to missionize and tyrannize everyone, many souls are broken, darkened, lost and immobilized. It is far better to *invite* people to join you in your belief than to threaten consequences if they will not.

Superordinate Goals

Preaching is a very effective teaching tool, but only in one area. By being preached at, people learn and incorporate self-hatred. It is a humorous but bitter irony that the American leadership in the 1980's told kids "just say no to drugs." Such a statement shows clearly how remote and ignorant about education and children our leadership can be and was during Reagan's time. "Just say no" was so peculiarly ironic because in every other context, school, home and church, we teach our kids night and day to "just say yes." As a matter of fact, that's about all they are taught. Saying "no" is taking an individual stand, and as I've tried to show repeatedly in this book, taking an individual stand is what Pathological Christianity cannot abide.

Expecting children to be successful and competent in any true sense requires a belief in their value as individuals. We demonstrate our belief in them by expecting them to be effective and competent, but not by determining the way in which they will do that, what particular outcomes should come of their actions or by giving them help they don't need. We can, however provide superordinate goals or help children find channels for their learning and practice and working together with others to accomplish tasks of meaning and value.

A simple example of superordinate goals at home is something like a twelve year old boy or girl to fix dinner for the family from planning the dinner to serving it to cleaning it up. The hardest thing for a parent in this situation is, perhaps, staying out of the way. Nor should a parent try to be too "helpful."

Young people can accomplish far more and expand their own horizons much farther if we will *allow them to do so*. We may say to kids, I expect you to contribute something to your community, to do something to help your neighbors; you can choose and discover *what* this is going to be, and work with other kids to make it come about, but you must do something. Most kids will find this a workable challenge and, with far less help than you might think (parents wish to think they are indispensable), they will make it happen.

We know that the most effective programs against gang violence or drugs among kids utilize the strength, knowledge and energy of kids themselves, and gives them a deep feeling of confidence. When kids themselves are guided to solve their own problems, it is far more effective than when adults try to move in and intervene on their own. Preaching never works.

Using Fear As a Teaching Tool

Fear can be divided into two categories, *practical fear* and *metaphysical fear*. Practical fear is simple. It is the kind of fear we need a dose of when we drive an automobile or engage in a dangerous sport, when we handle flammable liquids or when a tornado is coming across a field toward the house. The sensation of fear in these circumstances motivates us to do something immediate and specific to avoid a true, identifiable danger.

Metaphysical fear is different. It is the fear taught by Pathological Christianity. It takes the form of dread, of final, irredeemable punishment: the fear of God, the fear of Hell. It has no value whatsoever. It makes us dark, brooding, anxious, depressed. It does not stimulate people to do good. Doing good to avoid *ultimate* punishment is not, finally, of any value.

If a child gets punished because he rides his bicycle into the traffic, it is appropriate, because he can understand the reasonable, direct purpose of his punishment. It is wrong to tell a child that because he has sexual thoughts or rageful thoughts about his sister, God will hold it against him.

Religious and political leaders love to use *metaphysical fear*. They love to terrify. They like to use substitute words for *Satan*. These words can be anything, depending on the political climate--words like *liberalism, environmentalists, Republicans, homosexuals,* whoever is currently considered to be "the enemy." This serves only one function, which is to paralyze people from acting independently, and to force them into conformity.

Metaphysical fear is a method to try to keep people *babies*, waiting for salvation.

If you want a foolproof method to guarantee your child will need therapy, here is one. Tell him that God will punish him for being bad. Tell him in an angry tone of voice. To be more effective, tell him on the way to church.

Here is a second foolproof method. Tell your child that God will reward her and bless her if she *accepts Jesus Christ as her personal Lord and Savior*. Tell her this on the way home from church.

While you are at it, sprinkle in a few ethnic groups she should be afraid of. Tell her to watch out for men, who *obviously are only interested in one thing*. Tell her *men are really just children who never grow up, but once you marry one, you must serve him in the ways he needs, you must never leave him and yet must depend on him for protection, your sense of well-being, and to make the important decisions in outer life.*

Skills, Manual Labor, Crafts

Pathological Christianity depends on people to feel and act incompetent and confused about the world. One way to help children fight these effects is to give them many ways to be competent in their world, and be independent and anarchical. Show them how to refuse to pay outrageous prices for things they can do themselves, with training. Show them how to save money and how to stop depending on utility companies, mechanics, doctors and others, and restore them to competency.

People who know how to fix appliances, do simple wiring and carpentry, who understand the principles of insulation, septic systems, solar power and the like, have a particular place of independence that others who don't know such things cannot imagine. It is stupid to work for ten dollars an hour, pay a fourth of it to taxes, and then have the rest eaten up in services or goods that could be produced for far less than they cost by the time they have gone through several levels of "brokers," costs of doing business and the like.

Knowledge can be used to topple useless and obsolete institutions rather than to support them; it can be used to restore competence and confidence in people and their value in friendships and family. How much of any working person's day is spent earning money to support his incompetence at a job he despises? Given the cost of goods, services, groceries and taxes, hardly anyone who really looked at it could afford to work at the jobs they have. An alternative is to do work you love (even if it pays little), to keep a garden, work to unplug from the utilities companies, refuse to buy services or goods that keep you enslaved to institutions and credit card companies, pay only cash for anything you buy, and have the time and energy to pursue the things of most value to your soul: friendships, family relations, handwork, arts and crafts, gardening, things which feed soul rather than devouring it.

Children with manual skills as well as intellectual and social training have a good shot at autonomy in life. Children without such skills, even if they are very versed in some "school" information are bound to be enslaved. Children with skills will be less likely to knuckle under the pressure to feel narcissistically entitled and to parasite the nation, the taxpayers. As I have argued before in this book, narcissistic entitlement comes from enslavement to Pathological Christianity. When you teach conformity, mindlessness, the following of rules as a definition of "being good," you are producing parasites. Our schools must begin to see children as competent, and to prepare them for two things: the life of the mind, and practical, usable skills.

As it is now, schools teach neither one. They teach conformity and facts. A school with the purpose of creating autonomous, thinking, feeling individuals who have a chance at deep satisfaction throughout life will teach classical literature, mechanical skills, physical education (for life sports, not high school competition), and will have each student hooked up with a mentor, an older person in the community who is responsible for the children, like godparents once were.

Here are some other suggestions for infiltrating our institutions and helping
us understand and use the competence of individuals

Using Fathers

- Get fathers who are in jail to be involved directly with their children. We must begin to see that even jailed fathers are fathers, and that they have responsibilities to their children. Because we have for so long diminished the importance of fathers in the lives of children, we have disenfranchised them. Having fathers and mothers directly involved in the lives of their children, demanding this, can show that we believe in the competence of all people to do the right thing with their lives and their children. Often people are in jail for reasons that have more to do with political reasons than purely criminal ones (otherwise, the prisons would be full of defrauding white-collar workers from the financial institutions). Jailing people has been shown conclusively to have no good effect on their behavior, and is costly and goal-less; it comes out of a Pathological Christian view that we put people we don't like in a box and ignore them, or kill them. A far better, and ultimately more cost-effective and socially effective way to deal with people who are "criminals" would be to find ways to use whatever talents these people have and get them to use them.

- Stop gender bias and refusing the rights of fathers. Pathological Christianity has some bizarre view that child-rearing is woman's work, and therefore, men have been cut out of the family. Many men today feel awkward in child raising, but it is only because they have been cut out (like their fathers) from the expectation of direct involvement in child-rearing. *Men are innately equally as competent as women to raise children, and some men have more of the basic temperament to do so than some women.* Infiltrate Pathological Christianity by refusing "roles" in childrearing. The other side of the coin is that women are just as capable, innately, as men to make financial decisions, work in the corporation (if they should wish to, Godspeed!).

- Find models of resilience and strength in the family tree. A careful and honest review of family history will demonstrate talent and strength somewhere in a family, no matter what family we are looking at. When we look at these strengths and competencies honestly and without fear, we will discover coursing through our veins a source of individual competence and strength that will show us that we often need go no further than our own blood, psyche and family history to find particular strengths needed to create solutions to difficult problems. We don't need support groups, which encourage conformity, since we have that internally and somewhere in our own family history. There is enough variety and anarchy in any family to encourage each of us to find our own solutions to problems.

- Use a sense of humor about parenting, since it is only one part of the development of children. Don't be surprised when kids turn out vastly different than you were trying to program them to be. Pathological Christianity sees parenting as *serious business,* since the goal is to produce little soldiers for Christ. If you abandon this project, and begin to see that parenting is an experiment whose outcome you don't know and can't really and shouldn't predict, you can make parenting an experience of enjoyment rather than a *ministry.* All ministries, since they have a particular outcome in mind, are *bound to fail.*

- (continued from above) If your kid grows up to be an evangelical, realize that your Pathological Christianity is unconscious and stronger than you understand, and that it is something to be amused about.

Chapter 12. *The Spirituality of Direct Experience*

THE SPIRITUALITY OF DIRECT EXPERIENCE is a psyche-spirituality. It is not otherworldly. There is no higher, no lower, no in, no out. Both chaos and order are good and bad.

Direct spirituality is the immediate honoring of experience and a respectful attitude to the innumerable attempts to construe life that have arisen in all cultures at all times. It has no formalisms, no rituals, no leaders. It worships nothing above anything else, but everything at once. It finds everything holy and crazy.

Direct spirituality leaves all the unanswerable questions about such things as the creation of the world and what happens after death to the departments of creation and afterlife, though enjoys fooling around with these concepts. Direct spirituality is humble and posts no bills. When it builds a church, no one knows, because it is merely a well-constructed house or a tent by a river.

Direct spirituality eliminates the need to ask ultimate questions and finds Science just as funny as Televangelism. The practitioner of direct spirituality does not mention his "faith", but can just as well be present at a church meeting or not, and could even be on the Finance Committee of the Methodist Church if he is secretly grinning. He knows how to appear quite interested in churches or schools or other marvelous forms of human existence, but sees them all as equally worthy of respect and laughable, none any more than any other.

Direct spirituality is a lot cheaper and the extra money can be used to stop the construction of dams whose purpose is to halt the sexy wiggling of rivers, or it can be used to buy a seat on the Senate to create all sorts of intriguing confusion.

Faith, Direct and Indirect.

In the realm of Pathological Christianity, when you ask a difficult question, that is, a question that has no answer, you will get the answer, "you must accept this one on faith." Any time you hear that, know that you are getting a *cult* answer. Cults require the end of thinking.

Catechisms, or lists of "correct" answers to hard questions exist in all fields, whether religious, scientific or political. Certain questions demand answers even when there are none. It seems often that the most essential things in our lives are the things most impossible to understand yet which need answers, so we make answers.

This answer-making activity appears fundamental in the human personality, as ubiquitous as the question asking activity. Answer making itself is not bad, certainly, but there is a difference between *an* answer and *the* answer. Any time you hear that something is *the* answer, that's fundamentalism.

You cannot converse with a fundamentalist. Your choices are the following.

1. Listen. All fundamentalists love a *listener* above all. Third best is a respectful listener who doesn't mind being raved at. Second best is a cohort in agreement. But the very best of all is a *grateful convert*, a convert brought in and registered. The true jewel is the convert who was an ardent enemy. For what delights the fundamentalist above all is exercising power over the unwilling, kindling zeal in the unwashed, putting a notch in the old liturgical bedpost. Conversion is a form of feeding, a form of nutrition for the fundamentalist, the finest source of protein and vitamins.

2. Agree and encourage. Say *amen.* this form of exchange is agreeable to the fundamentalist, but more in the

spirit of shepherding the flock. It's maintenance work. It does, however, provide ongoing income, so the amen-sayers are valuable, if only as breed stock.

3. Go to war. The fundamentalist would almost as soon have an enemy as a convert. Fighting is a vivid direct demonstration of loyalty and seriousness. It is a great way to make a point, prove one's righteousness and avoid the tiresome activity of thinking.

Now what about faith? Doesn't everybody need faith in some form. After all, there is enough in life to feel uncertain about, don't we need something or somebody to believe in?

One kind of faith is actually the expression of a psychological need or wish that there be a form of magic that conforms to my needs and will grant me what it is that I most need, even if I can't figure them out. Unfortunately many marriages are based on this kind of delusional faith. But in Pathological Christianity, there is a catch, which is that God will grant my needs (as he did in the Garden of Eden) if I don't look behind the curtain, question God or become *willful*. The requirement is that we not ask or if we do ask we do so in a very specific way, recognizing that answers have already been given and that I merely need pray, study Bible and get more humbly and fervently behind Jesus to get clear on the answers. Scripture is a done deal, frozen in the ice of the Bible in unchanging and unchangeable forms.

Another kind of faith is found in direct spirituality. Here faith is an acceptance that there is a reality beyond what I can define, but by definition I won't be able to define it, recognize it, know it or explain it. I can feel confident however that there is some ultimate significance in life, because it is far more satisfying to feel that there is. Thinking that nothing means anything gives you a headache, though not as bad as thinking that everyone else knows the meaning and somewhere you missed it or weren't given the combination to get in, or were too stupid to try.

I don't have to or want to justify the beautiful complexity of life, worry about the future, convert anybody. That's God's job, and most likely he's equipped. My job is to be myself, protect the lustrous rivers and mountains from Pathological Christianity, practice courtesy and respect with my neighbors, be a decent friend to those I love, and tell the truth the best I can today, knowing that by tomorrow's standards I will likely be a ludicrous liar and fool.

One Final Bid for the Individual

The individual is the measure of all things. The "collective mind" knows nothing. I learned this from Christ.

Pathological Christianity has confused and undermined our understanding of the individual.

We must not confuse individualism with egotism, as is so often done. There is no reason to believe that one who thinks, feels and acts on his own is "irresponsible," just as there is no reason to believe that someone who "works for the common good" is responsible.

Some of the biggest egotists that have ever lived were "working for the common good."

When we teach ourselves and our children to respect individual thinking, feeling and action and to challenge and refute fundamentalisms where they steal the individual's soul, we teach the ultimate altruism.

Fundamentalisms chain and murder the soul. The soul delights and lives in freedom and autonomy.

INDEX

A

absolute parent, 128
abstinence, 153, 181
Adam, 209
advertising, 13, 21, 42, 45,
    87, 89, 123, 170,
    229
agoraphobia, 222
anger, 7, 93, 94, 95, 170,
    181, 203
anti-environmentalism, 211
anti-science attitude, 78
apocalypses, 218-220
art, 104, 110, 129, 189, 236
athletes, 204, 212
autominister, 128, 149

B

babies, 90, 122ff, 156, 221,
    233, 252
belief, varieties of, 208
Bible, 220, 225, 236, 249
Biblical models for men,
    197ff
Biblical models for women,
    200ff
Biblical principles, 8, 9, 112,
    162
bigotry, 25, 68, 204
Buddha, 105, 124, 169, 249

C

Calvinism, 203
capitalism, 203
certainty, cost of, 86
Cherry, 1531
children, 238ff
children's literature,
    Christian, 83
Christian Depth Psychology,
    162, 164ff
Christian Dualism, 75
Christian Men's Group, 188
Christian Psychology, 157ff,
    199, 220, 221, 249
Christian Woman, 46, 94,
    180, 190, 194, 200,
    203, 207
church tribunal, 193
Classical Education, 159
colonization, 45
communism, 205
Company Store, 92
conditioning, pathological,
    87ff
control, 62
conversion, 100. 126
critical feeling, 237
critical thinking, 237
cult defined, 39

DATE DUE
